Using
Quattro Pro 3

Using
Quattro Pro 3

P. K. McBride

NEWTECH

Newtech
An imprint of Butterworth-Heinemann Ltd
Linacre House, Jordan Hill, Oxford OX2 8DP

 PART OF REED INTERNATIONAL BOOKS

OXFORD   LONDON   BOSTON
MUNICH   NEW DELHI   SINGAPORE   SYDNEY
TOKYO   TORONTO   WELLINGTON

First published 1991

British Library Cataloguing in Publication Data
A CIP catalogue record for this book is available from
the British Library

ISBN 0 7506 0358 5

Produced by Butford Technical Publishing
Butford Farm, Bodenham, Hereford
Printed and bound in Great Britain by
Biddles Ltd, Guildford and King's Lynn

Contents

Contents

Contents

PART ONE

Getting started

■ SECTION 1
Introducing Quattro Pro

Over the past few years, Borland have established themselves as a leading supplier of programming languages and applications software. In Quattro Pro 3, the latest version of their successful worksheet, they have a product that is well capable of matching – and in some respects surpassing – the market leader in this field. It has an impressive combination of power, adaptability and ease of use, and offers a vast range of facilities. The key features are so simple to understand and to use, that it should be possible to put the system to work in earnest within an hour or so of starting. Yet it has the capacity to handle the most complex and sophisticated applications.

Like all worksheets, Quattro Pro is, in essence, a large grid of boxes (*cells* in the jargon) in which you can write text, numbers or formulae that will process those numbers. It is a general-purpose tool, a combination notepad, reference table and calculator, that can be used in an almost unlimited number of ways. Financial modelling – budgeting, forecasting and analysis – is an obvious area of use, and most major Quattro applications will be of this type. Other obvious uses are in the fields of statistical and scientific analysis. Quattro's large size and its varied set of built-in functions – which make light work of complex calculations – allow it to cope easily with any kind of mathematical modelling task.

But there is potential for far more varied work. It has many desktop publishing features, allowing you to create enhanced text displays on screen and on paper. No more boring printouts, when it takes only a few keystrokes to add lines and boxes, shades and highlights, and a range of type styles and sizes. The worksheet that manages the sales and the stock can also print out a snappy invoice and a crisp catalogue.

Quattro's graphic facilities are more developed than those of any other spreadsheet system currently on the market. It doesn't just produce annotated graphs, it gives you a full presentation graphics system. You can draw your own images or import them from clip-art files; combine graphs, pictures and text freely and to excellent effect; and link sets of screens to create a 'slide show'.

Database management facilities make up a fourth major part of the Quattro system. They are by no means as comprehensive as those that you would find in a proper database package, but it has been my experience that for some types of data processing, it is more convenient to use this spreadsheet than a standard database. Editing, searching, sorting, adding and deleting records can all be managed quickly and easily. Where more advanced processing is required, the data can be exported in a suitable form with just a few keystrokes – and the combination of Quattro Pro and Borland's companion database, Paradox, gives very powerful data-handling capabilities.

And there's still more! Quattro Pro has enough word-processing facilities to allow you to write a simple report directly around your tables and calculations – parts of this book were originally written in the worksheet; there's a good file manager utility tucked into the command set; and its macro programming language lets you automate and simplify the operation of the sheets, so that even those with virtually no understanding of the system can enter data and output results.

Quattro Pro was designed to be as easy as possible to use. The trouble is, it wasn't just designed to be easy for novices, but also for those who are used to working with Lotus 1-2-3 and similar spreadsheet systems, and for those used to working with Windows and mice. As a result, there are often two or three ways of achieving the same end! In an effort to avoid confusion, I shall only mention the alternatives when they first crop up – so that you know they are there – and afterwards will stick to the mainstream methods.

■ SECTION 1
Introducing Quattro Pro

The focus of this book is on using Quattro Pro in a business
context. The commands and features of the system are explored
and explained, but as far as possible this is within realistic –
though simplified – applications. I haven't attempted to cover every
single option of every single feature. It is simply not possible in a
book of this size. Instead, I have followed the 99% rule, and tried
to cover those things that 99% of users will want 99% of the time.

■ SECTION 2
The screen and the worksheet

Any spreadsheet screen can be a little daunting if it is the first time you have ever met one, and Quattro Pro is no different from the rest in this respect. So let's see what it's all about.

The bulk of the screen is taken up by an expanse of blank space (Figure 2.1). This is in fact a grid of cells, each one of which can contain a separate item of data. The columns and rows are marked by letters across the top and numbers down the left side. These are used to identify the cells. The cell references are always written column letter first, so A1 refers to the top left cell; C15, the cell in column C at row 15.

The cells are initially nine characters wide, but the width can be varied at will, and the cell's contents are not limited by the displayed width, as you will see in Section 4.

One of these cells will be highlighted (red on a colour monitor). This is the current cell: the one into which data can be entered.

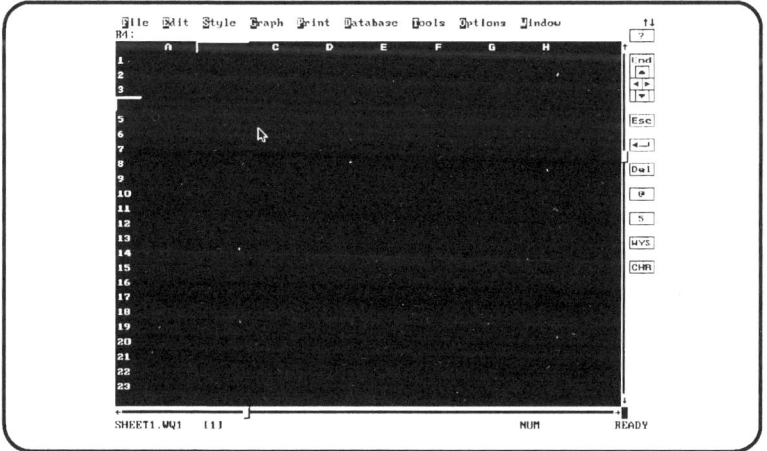

Figure 2.1

■ SECTION 2
The screen and the worksheet

You will see that its column letter and row number are likewise highlighted. Mouse users will also notice a small highlighted (black and orange) block. This will appear as an arrow if you have an EGA or VGA monitor, and have selected the graphics display mode – one of the options that we will look at later.

What is displayed on screen is only a window onto the grid – a very small part of its potential size. Those column letters go to Z, then carry on AA, AB, AC, ... through to AZ, BA, BB, ... and on to IV – that's 255 columns in all. Go far enough down and you will eventually hit bottom at row 8192. This gives you a total of 2,088,960 cells in the grid. That should be enough for most purposes! In practice, you could never actually fill them all, as you would run out of memory along the way. However, you may want to write very wide, or very long sheets, or to spread yourself, allowing lots of empty space around each separate part of a complex sheet.

To the immediate right and below this window onto the grid are the scroll bars – shaded bars with bright white on red indicator boxes. These boxes show the position of the cursor in relation to the whole sheet. Mouse users can move rapidly over the sheet by dragging these boxes along the bars. The symbols in the corners of the borders are also used for mouse control, as is the palette on the extreme right of the sheet. (If you haven't got a mouse, there's just a black strip here instead.) We will look further at mouse and keyboard control in the next section.

Along the top line of the screen are the names of the commands sets.

```
File  Edit  Style  Graph  Print  Database  Tools  Options  Window
```

■ SECTION 2
The screen and the worksheet

Each of these gives access to a pull-down menu, each containing a set of related commands, many of which have their own sub-menus of options. Though there are in total a great number of commands, the well-organised structure of menus makes them very easy to find and use.

The second line at the top of the screen is for data entry. If you are used to word processing rather than spreadsheeting, the way that you get data into the system can come as a bit of a surprise. You don't write directly onto the sheet. Instead, you move the highlighted cursor to the cell into which you want to write, then type the data into the entry line. There's good reason for this. In word processing there is only one type of data: text. In a spreadsheet there are two types: Labels (or text) and Values, which can be subdivided into simple numbers and calculating formulae. The system must be able to distinguish between them, and – very importantly – it must be able to check that formulae are written in a way that it can understand. By filtering all data through the entry line, these checks can be managed more easily. In the same way, when you want to alter the contents of a cell, it is first pulled up onto this line, and edited there.

Once you start to get data into the system, you will see that the entry line has another function. As the cursor moves over the screen, this line displays the contents of the current cell, its width – if it has been changed – and other information.

At the very bottom of the screen is the status line. What is displayed here depends largely upon what you are doing at the time. Generally it will show the name of the active sheet and its number, the status of the Caps, Scroll and Number Lock keys, and the current mode of operation. (Date and time can also be displayed here if you choose.) When you are working through the command menus, brief descriptions of the commands are shown here; and when you are editing a cell's contents, the original contents are displayed here, so that you can refer back to them if necessary.

Modes of operation and the mode indicator are worth a brief mention at this point. When the spreadsheet is waiting for you to give a command or enter data, it will indicate this by a 'READY' at the bottom left of the screen. As you start to write data into a cell, the mode indicator will change to either 'LABEL' or 'VALUE', depending upon what you are writing. When editing the contents of a cell, you will see 'EDIT' down there, and when accessing the command set, the indicator shows 'MENU'. There are other modes, but we can forget about them for the time being.

If you have a colour monitor and don't like the colours of the screen, that presents no problem. As with much else of the Quattro system, these can be tailored to your taste. Personally, I like the basic combination of red, white and blue for the main working screen, but have brought in some additional splashes of colour to highlight menus, and have redesigned some of the other parts of the system. Changing the screen colours is covered in Section 50.

■ SECTION 3
The keyboard and the mouse

Movement around the screen

This is all largely intuitive – if you do what feels right, it will normally work! However, there are a few occasions where intuition is not enough.

Keyboard control

Intuitive keys are:

[Arrow] keys	One cell in the direction of the arrow
[PgUp] [PgDn]	One screen depth up and down
[Home]	Move to the top left cell (A1)

Almost intuitive keys are:

[Ctrl]+[Left] or [Tab]	One screen width left
[Ctrl]+[Right] or [Shift]+[Tab]	One screen width right

Idiosyncratic keys are:

[End] followed by [Arrow]	Next end of block
[End] followed by [Home]	Bottom right cell of active sheet

Strange things can happen after you have pressed the [End] key. There is no immediate effect – no movement – except that the word 'END' pops up into the status line at the bottom of the screen. But if you then press an arrow key, the cursor leaps to the end of the nearest block of occupied cells, in the direction of the arrow. Now 'end' here can mean either the near or the far end. If the cursor is in a block of cells, the jump is to the far end, otherwise it is to the start of the next block. And if there are no more occupied cells in that direction, it leaps to the far end of the sheet. The technique is quite handy for leaping about within a solid block of occupied cells, but as a means of moving quickly about the sheet, it has its drawbacks.

Mouse control

Intuitive options are:

■   Click on the arrows on the mouse palette, to move the cursor one cell at a time.

■   To relocate the highlight bar within the visible page, move the pointer to the desired cell and click the left button.

■   To move to another part of the larger (off-screen) sheet, use the right-hand and bottom scroll bars. Either drag the indicator box by pointing to it, holding down the left button and moving the mouse; or click on the arrows at the ends of the bars to move the screen window 20 rows or a full width in the required direction.

■   The HOME button on the mouse palette acts the same as the [Home] key.

Idiosyncratic options include the END button, which has the same effect as the [End] key. Click on this, then on an arrow button, and the cursor leaps to the next end of a block. Follow it with a click on the HOME button, and you move to the bottom right of the sheet.

Function keys
The function keys, used by themselves or in combination with [Shift] and [Alt], give access to 24 different features. Borland thoughtfully include a keyboard reminder strip in the Quattro package. We'll take them one by one as they are needed.

Don't panic!
When things go wrong, it will be comforting to know that there are three keys that will probably let you get it back together again.

[F1]   Calls up the on-screen help system. (See Section 8 for details.)

[Alt]+[F5]   Undo; takes you back to where you were before the last operation.

[Esc]   Cancels what you are doing. If you have inadvertently strayed into the wrong part of the command menus, it takes you back out, one stage at a time. If you are in danger of writing the wrong thing into a cell, it scraps whatever is in the entry line, leaving the cell as it was before.

■ SECTION 4
Numbers and calculations

First and foremost a spreadsheet is a number-cruncher. Anything else it does may well be useful, but it is incidental. So, how do we get numbers into it, how does it handle them, and how do we perform calculations?

Numbers
Entering numbers is normally very straightforward. Move the cursor to the cell in which the number is to be written, then type in the digits. The word 'VALUE' appears in the mode indicator slot at the bottom right of the screen, and the digits appear in the entry line at the top of the screen. When you have finished, press [Return] and the number will be transferred to the current cell.

Oops!
If you make a mistake while entering the number, use the [Backspace] key – the left arrow on the top right of the main set – to erase back to the error. If you change your mind after you have started – it's the wrong number or in the wrong place – press [Escape] to abandon the entry. *Don't use punctuation.* Type in commas to separate the thousands – e.g. 12,345,678 – and Quattro will beep at you and flash the message 'Error Invalid Character'. If this happens, press [Escape] to clear the error message, then either erase back to correct it or [Escape] and start again.

Appearance and reality
Unless you choose to set a specific style – and we'll get back to that in Section 15 – numbers will normally be displayed on screen just as you entered them. You can see some examples in Figure 4.1. Notice how they are justified to the right; i.e. pushed across the cell so that the final digit is on the right-hand side. This is normally how you would want numbers to appear, especially where there is a column of values with the total at bottom. As long

Numbers and calculations

```
         A          B              C
1    Simple numbers       20 Characters wide
2
3            1                123,456,789,012
4          123            123,456,789,012,345
5       12.345            1.2345678901235E+16
6      0.12345
7     1.23E+09
8
```

Figure 4.1

as all the values have the same number of decimals, right justification will put the decimal points in line.

Very long numbers may appear to pose a problem. If there isn't
room in the cell for all the digits, then the number will be displayed
in exponential – or scientific – format. Enter the ten-digit number
1234567890 into a standard nine-character width cell and you
get:

    1.23E+09

To convert this back to a proper value, take the decimal value on
the left and multiply it by 10 to the power of the number on the
right. In this case 1.23 * 10^9, or 1.23 * 1,000,000,000. (Divide it
by 10 to the power if there is a minus sign before the number.)

It is worth noting that there may well be a difference between what
you see on the screen and what is actually held in a cell. A number
may appear to have lost a lot of digits – and therefore accuracy –
but this is only its display. Make the column wide enough and the
number will be shown in its full-digit finery. (Changing column
widths is covered in Section 15.)

■SECTION 4
Numbers and calculations

There's a limit of course. Quattro Pro can handle numbers with up to fifteen digits with full accuracy. Any more digits than this, and the later ones are rounded off; e.g. 12345678901234567 would be held internally as 1.2345678901235 * 10^16 and displayed, at best, as 12,345,678,901,235,000. I can think of few occasions where such loss of accuracy would be significant. In financial terms, it is equivalent to forgetting the pennies in a budget of thousands of billions of pounds.

Calculations

This difference between a cell's actual contents and its screen display has a very positive side to it. Write a calculation in a cell, and the result appears on screen. As long as you are only using numbers, the calculations don't have to be written in any special way – just follow the normal mathematical rules. For example:

Contents	Display	Comments
2+2	4	What else?
3*4	12	Note the use of * for multiply
2+3*4	14	Multiplication performed before addition
(2+3)*4	20	Anything in brackets calculated first
3^2	9	^ means 'to the power of'

There's a bit more to it when you include cell references or functions in your formulae, as we shall see in the next section.

Labels

In Quattro Pro, any kind of text is referred to as a 'label'. I find this slightly misleading. True, most bits of text will probably act as labels – headings on tables of figures, notes by individual items of data – but the word 'label' implies a limitation that isn't really there. A text item can be anything up to 255 characters long – that's over four lines of this book! And with the crude but effective word-processing facilities, it is possible to write solid pages of text within the worksheet.

In most cases, you can put text into a cell simply by moving the cursor to it and typing the words. Quattro will recognise that this is text as soon as you type the first letter, and the word 'LABEL' will appear in the Mode Indicator slot at the bottom right of the screen.

Justification

When you enter the text into the cell, you may notice that an apostrophe has been inserted at the start. This isn't visible in the cell – only in the entry line, where the contents of the current cell are automatically displayed. What is visible is its effect. That apostrophe specifies that the text is justified to the left; i.e. the first character of the label will be on the left of the cell. This may not be how you want it. If you have a multi-column table of (right-justified) numbers, it is easier to relate the headings to their columns if the labels are also justified to the right. To specify the justification, type one of these symbols at the start of the text:

Symbol	Justification
' (apostrophe)	Left
" (quote marks)	Right
^ (caret)	Centre

You can see examples of these in rows 6 to 8 in Figure 5.1.

SECTION 5
Text in the worksheet

```
            A            B
1   Text on the spreadsheet
2                    |
3   LABELS           |
4                    |
5     Justification  |
6   'Left            |
7             "Right |
8         ^Centre    |
9                    |
10  Long Entries     |
11  Can flow into the next cell
12   .. as long as  |OCCUPIED
13                   |
14                   |
15  Number text      |
16  '071-123-4567    |
```

Figure 5.1

Over-long labels

Where a text entry is longer that its cell's width, it will overflow –
on screen – onto the adjacent cells to the right, as long as these
are empty. In Figure 5.1, cell A11 contains Can flow into the
next cell, and the display does so. The label in A12, on the other
hand – .. as long as it is empty – is only partially displayed.
The word OCCUPIED in B12 blocks the flow.

Over-long right- and centre-justified labels behave in exactly the
same way as those that are left-justified, always spilling across to
the right.

Numbers as text

These need a bit of forethought. If you try and write in the address
10 Downing Street, Quattro spots the 10 and classes the entry
as a VALUE. It is then thrown by the words that come later. Phone
numbers can be even worse. Type in 071-123-4567, and Quattro
displays –4619. It's done the sum! If you have an entry that starts
with a number, and you want it treated as a label, then type an
apostrophe – or other justification symbol – at the start.

■ SECTION 6
Cell references and formulae

Single cell references

We noted in Section 2 that cells are identified by their column letter and row number, in the form A1, B42, Z80. Used in a formula, the reference will collect whatever value is currently held in that cell.

The simplest form of reference is where you want to copy a value from one part of a sheet to another – for reference, or to draw the results of different calculations together onto one screen. For these, you must write the cell reference *preceded by a + sign*, for example +A11, +B42. If A6 contains 3, any cell holding the reference +A6 displays the contents of A6, which is 3. Text values can be copied across in just the same way. If A4 has the label 'Hello Mum!' any cell containing +A4 will display that message.

Notes: **1** (The bad news): If you omit the + sign, the system will think that the reference is a piece of text, and will just display the reference – not the contents of the cell.

2 (The good news): Quattro doesn't mind if you use small or capital letters for the references.

References in formulae

When writing formulae to perform calculations, a cell reference can be used in any place where you would otherwise write a value. And the advantages of references over given values are readily seen.

Suppose you wanted to calculate the VAT due on an item costing £4.00. You could write the formula:

```
4*0.175
```

Cell references and formulae

It would give you the answer. But if you wanted a second VAT amount, you would have to write a second formula. Far easier to write the item value into a cell – say A2 – and use its reference in the formula:

```
+A2*0.175
```

Now when you want another VAT amount, it is only necessary to enter the item value into A2. You can take this a step further:

```
        A          B
1    VAT RATE    0.175
2    ITEM          4
3    VAT DUE      0.7        .... B3 = +B1*B2
```

VAT rates change – this section is being written on Budget Day, and the VAT rate has changed since I started writing. By putting the VAT Rate and the item value in cells, and referring to them in the formula, there is no need to rewrite the formula if either value changes.

Blocks of cells

There are many occasions within Quattro when you will perform an operation on a block of cells. These may be within a function – to find the sum, average or some other statistical result from a set of numbers – or within a command, where you are selecting a set of cells to be manipulated in some fashion. In all cases, the set is defined by giving the cell references of any two opposite corners, with the references separated by two full stops.

For example:

```
A1..A10    Cells 1 to 10 in column A
C5..F5     Cells on Row 5, from C to F
```

■ SECTION 6
Cell references and formulae

```
A1..C6 ⎫
C1..A6 ⎪   All refer to the same block, from A1 in
A6..C1 ⎬   the top left to C6 in the bottom right
C6..A1 ⎭
```

Let's sees how a cell block might be used.

@SUM – the first function
Quattro has a plethora of functions – ready-made routines for performing complex calculations – and most of them can be safely left until later. But there is one that is extremely useful, and which demonstrates nicely how a function works and how convenient they can be.

SUM will add up all the values in a given block. Like all functions it must be written with an @ sign at the front – to tell Quattro that it *is* a function. As this function works on a block of cells, the references must be given and are enclosed in brackets.

```
@SUM(A1..A6)
```

This gives the total of all the values in cells A1 to A6. It is equivalent to the formula:

```
+A1+A2+A3+A4+A5+A6
```

... but takes a fraction of the time to write. And there is also a hidden advantage. If you later decide that you want to include more values in the sum, you can insert additional rows between 1 and 6, and the block references will stretch to accommodate the new rows. Insert a new row 4, and @SUM(A1..A6) will become @SUM(A1..A7) without any work on your part. If you had used a +A1+A2+A3.. formula, you would have had to rewrite it. (The Insert command is covered in Section 13.)

■ SECTION 6
Cell references and formulae

Pointed references

As an alternative to writing cell references, you can point to them
– it's usually easier, often quicker and always more reliable.
There's nothing to it. Look back to the VAT calculation. To write
the formula +B1*B2 using the pointing method, you would go
through these steps:

1   Move to B3, the cell that will hold the formula.

2   Type + to start it off. The system is now expecting a value
or a reference.

3   Move the worksheet cursor towards B1. As it moves, it picks
up the reference of the cell under the cursor – first B2, then
B1 – and writes it into the entry line. Stop on the target cell.

4   Type * for the next operation.

5   Move the cursor again to pick up the reference to B2.

6   Press [Return] to tell Quattro that you have done. The
completed formula is transferred to B3.

The block reference for the formula @SUM(A1..A6) can also be
obtained by pointing. The sequence would be as follows:

1   Type the function name and opening bracket:

■ SECTION 6
Cell references and formulae

```
@SUM(
```

2 Quattro is expecting a reference. Point to A1.

3 Press [.]. This fixes one end of the block and prepares for the other. The formula will now read:

```
@SUM(A1..A1
```

4 Move to the other end. The highlighted area spreads and the second reference changes:

```
@SUM(A1..A6
```

5 Type the closing bracket and press [Return] to transfer the formula to the sheet.

In the next section we'll point to references for commands.

■ SECTION 7
Calling up commands

All of the commands in the Quattro system are available from the top menu line, and all follow set patterns of use. In practice, it means that once you have found your way around the first half dozen or so, the rest fall into place pretty easily. As long as you know that the command is there, and you know what it is supposed to do, actually making it work is rarely a problem. There are very few nasty surprises in this system.

Using the command menus

File	Edit	Style	Graph	Print	Database	Tools	Options	Window

Each keyword in that top line will open up to reveal a menu of commands. What happens next depends upon the nature of the command. With some, you simply select the command and that's it. On the Edit menu in Figure 7.1, you will see 'Undo'. Select this and it will instantly restore your worksheet to how it was before you made a mess of it! Some commands require further input from you. 'Edit Copy' will want to know which cells to copy where. Other commands have options that are controlled by a further level of menus. In 'Edit Delete', for example, there is then a choice between 'Rows' and 'Columns' (see Figure 7.1).

There are a variety of ways in which you can select commands – this is one area of Quattro where you are spoiled for choice. They are all easy to use, so if I simply list them, you can try them out and pick the method that suits you. While you are doing this, have a browse around to see what is on offer. Notice that as the highlight bar passes over a name, a brief description of the command appears in the very bottom line of the screen.

Calling up commands

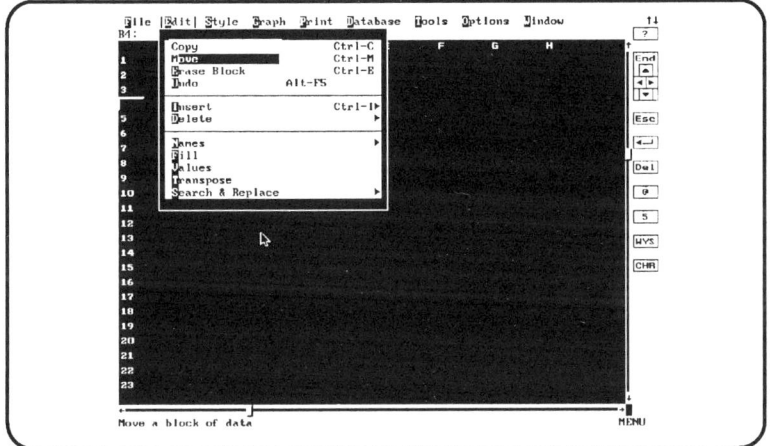

Figure 7.1

The mouse

This is probably the easiest method of all – if you have a mouse and space to run it in.

Point to the name in the top line menu and click (left button). The menu appears. Point to the command name and click. You may then have to click to select from further levels of menus, or supply cell references or other data.

The keyboard

This is a two stage operation, with alternatives at each stage. The first job is to activate the top line menu, and that can be done by pressing either of two keys:

[/]   Forward slash, usually by the right [Shift] key

[F3]   The function key that Quattro calls 'Choices'

■ SECTION 7
Calling up commands

File, the first of the set names, will be highlighted to indicate that the menu is active. The very bottom line of the screen will now display a brief description of the nature of the commands in this set.

There are two ways to select a command set from the top line, and the same alternatives apply when you come to select from the menus:

■ Type the highlighted letter – usually the initial. This is the quickest method, as long as you know your way round the keyboard.

■ Move the highlight bar to the command name with the cursor keys – left and right on the top line, up and down on the menus – and press [Return] when it is on the chosen one.

Commands and references

Many of the commands require cell or block references, and it is usually easiest to give these by pointing. Here's one of the simplest: Edit l Erase. It's purpose is to wipe cells clean.

Pull down the Edit menu and select Erase. A prompt will appear up in the entry line:

```
Block to be modified:C5..C5
```

The cell references will be those of the current cell. Quattro is assuming that you will want to wipe a block of cells, and that the current cell will be at one corner of this block. Move the cursor and the second reference will change, while highlights spread over the area between the references. Try it, and you will see that you can spread the block in any direction, always pivoting around the current cell.

If you want to erase a cell or block elsewhere on the sheet, press [Escape]. This removes the references from the prompt line. Move the cursor, and its reference will pop into the line. If you only want to erase a single cell, point to that cell, then press [Return] to complete the command. For a block, point to a corner then press [.]. This fixes the first reference and starts the second. Spread the highlight area to cover the block and press [Return].

Shortcuts and function keys

Some of the more frequently used commands have been given keyboard shortcuts – you can call them up by pressing [Ctrl] and a letter key. You are more likely to make mistakes this way, than by selecting from a visible menu, but they can speed up operations once you have learnt them.

In Figure 7.1 you will see that 'Copy' has 'Ctrl-C' beside it, and that several others in this set also have 'Ctrl-...' equivalents. About a dozen key combinations have been defined already, and the system allows you to set up your own in the same way. You may wish to glance ahead to Section 49, which looks at shortcuts and how to create them.

A few commands are also duplicated on the function keys. These are given on the keyboard overlay in the Quattro package. You may well find, as I do, that it is as quick to select from the menus as to look up the correct combination of [Shift], [Alt] and function key.

Oops!

If you have got into the wrong part of the menu system, you can back up to the previous level of menu by pressing [Escape] – or move off the menu and click, with the mouse. If you select the wrong command – and it has been carried out – follow up immediately with Edit I Undo (or press [Alt]-[F5]). This will put the sheet back to as it was before that command.

■ SECTION 8
Instant Help

Help is never far away, although it is not always a great deal of use. Still, every little helps. To get into the Help system, at any time – whatever you are doing – simply press [F1].

The system is context-sensitive, which means that the help screen that is displayed will be related to what you were doing at the time. If the sheet is in READY mode – i.e. waiting for you to stop messing about and do something – then the displayed screen is 'Help Topics', the main menu for the system. If you are in the process of making a selection from the command menus, then Help will tell you about the command that is highlighted at the time. If you are typing in a formula or some data, Help will tell you how to use the cursor keys for editing.

In all cases, the screen will give you links to other parts of the Help system. Somewhere on the page there will be keywords picked out by reverse printing or by a different colour. Move the highlight bar to the appropriate word and press [Return] to open up the related Help screen. There is almost always a direct route back to 'Help Topics', and from there you can get to any other part of the system.

Press [F1] and have a dip into it. It's well worth knowing what is available, and getting the feel of how it works. I think that the Help pages are clearly written and well organised, if rather uninspiring in appearance. What they lack are examples. This is a shame, as some concepts are very difficult to grasp without examples. On the other hand, if the Help system were better, perhaps fewer people would feel the need to buy books about Quattro ...

PART TWO

Creating a worksheet

■ SECTION 9
The basic design

This section covers some of the key commands and techniques, and in the process shows how to create a simple budgeting system. Here, as in most of the rest of the book, I'm assuming that you will be trying out the examples in Quattro as you read.

Budget management
One of the most common uses for a spreadsheet in business is budget management. It is relatively straightforward to set up – certainly no more complex than performing the same job on paper – and the benefits are clearly worth the effort of making the transition from paper. Not only will it do all the totalling and calculations for you, it will keep on doing them as you revise and refine the original budget.

The budgeting process starts by setting realistic targets for income and expenditure for the next financial period – typically a monthly breakdown over a year. Once into the year, actual income and expenditure can be compared with the budgetary plan, and action taken quickly if it becomes clear that targets are not being met. Far better to nip an overspend in the bud than to have a major cashflow crisis suddenly loom at you out of the mists.

What follows is a very simplified system, but the principle remains the same, no matter how many sub-categories of income and expenditure.

A worksheet should start its life on paper. I know there's a great temptation to just start typing it straight onto the screen, but really the time you spend planning a new worksheet is time well spent. As you will see shortly, it is perfectly possible to re-organise a sheet – moving chunks from one place to another, inserting new rows, even turning tables on their heads. It is all possible – but it is quicker and easier to do it right first time! So let's get planning.

The basic design

It is not worth doing a complete cell-by-cell plan of the whole sheet, but we do need to establish the overall layout and the relationships between the various sets of figures. Our simple budget will cover sales and expenses over a period of six months. That gives us two dimensions – budget categories and time – and therefore falls naturally into a table form. Which way should we lay the table out? With the time line across the top or down the side? It won't make any difference to the calculations, but presentation and readability are important.

The answer depends upon the number of divisions in each dimension. Though there are only two categories of sales and five of expenses, totals and profit and balance calculations will increase the number of category headings to over ten. Against this, there will only be six months and a total along the time line. As there are more visible rows than columns on a screen, we'll set the table with the categories in the rows and the time line across the top.

Our firm has two sales lines. One product sells steadily, earning around £10,000 per month. The second is newly introduced but has been well received by customers. The marketing manager forecasts that sales should rise steadily from £6,000 in January up to £16,000 by the end of the half year.

Expenses can be grouped under five headings. Three of these are directly related to production – and therefore sales. Material costs are equivalent to 30% of sales, labour to 25% and commission to 5%. (The real world time-lags between outlay and income have been ignored!) Overheads generally run at £4,000 per month, and power costs should be £3,500 per month during the winter quarter, dropping to around £3,000 in spring.

These figures and the relationships between them have been written out in Figure 9.1. Let's get them into a worksheet.

```
                Jan    Feb    March   April   May    June   Total
Sales A         Steady 10,000 per month
Sales B         New product - projected sales 6,000 rising to 16,000
TOTAL IN        Sales A + Sales B

EXPENSES
Materials       30% of Sales
Labour          25% of Sales
Commission      5% of Sales
Overheads       4,000 per month on average
Power           3,500 per month winter; 3,000 spring
TOTAL OUT       Add all expenses

Profit/Loss     IN - OUT

Balance         Add profit/loss to current balance
                Initial overdraft 10,000
```

Figure 9.1

Starting a new sheet

If you have just got Quattro up and running and the system is still clear of data, then skip the next few lines. Otherwise, clear the decks for action.

From the **File** menu, select **Erase** to wipe the sheet clean. If there are any entries anywhere, you will be prompted:

```
Lose your Data?
```

Select **Yes** to confirm the Erase.

Headings

Enter headings first, so that the structure is clearly visible. Leaving blank rows or columns between different sets of items will help to improve the readability of the sheet. The title in the Home cell (A1), is optional.

Write the headings into the cells as follows – and please stick to the same cells, or you'll have problems with cell references later. Move the cursor to the given cell and type the contents into the entry line. When you finish each entry *don't press [Return]*! Instead, press the arrow key in the direction of the next cell. The data will be transferred to the sheet and the cursor will move on with a single keypress.

Don't worry about the fact that some headings are wider than their cells – the extra characters will overflow into the next column as long as it is blank. We'll leave column B blank.

Don't worry about minor typing errors. If you make a major error – or write in the wrong cell – press [Escape] to abandon the entry and start again. If you enter something into the wrong cell, then either write over it or ignore it. We'll tidy things up later.

```
A1:  Budget - First Half Year
C3:  Jan
D3:  Feb
...  etc. to ...
H3:  June
I3:  Total
A4:  Sales A
A5:  Sales B
A6:  TOTAL IN
A8:  EXPENSES
A9:  Materials
A10: Labour
A11: Commission
A12: Overheads
A13: Power
```

```
A15:  TOTAL OUT
A17:  Profit/Loss
A19:  Balance
```

Values and formulae

The numbers on this sheet are a mixture of actual values and calculations. At this point, only enter those for January: column C. Notice how the formulae are translated almost directly from the written descriptions in Figure 9.1. (Check back to Section 6 if you need any help with the cell references.)

```
C4:  10000           {Sales A}
C5:  6000            {Sales B}
C6:  +C4+C5          {Sales A + Sales B}
C9:  0.3*C6          {30% of TOTAL IN}
C10: 0.25*C6         {25% ...}
C11: 0.05*C6         {5% ...}
C12: 4000
C13: 3500
C15: @SUM(C9..C13)   {Add up all the expenses}
C17: +C6-C15         {TOTAL IN - TOTAL OUT}
```

The running Balance across row 19 creates a minor problem. It is normally calculated by adding the Profit/Loss to the previous month's Balance, but January doesn't have a 'previous month'. The simplest solution is to write the overdraft of -10000 in column B, and work from there.

```
B19: -10000
C19: +B19+C17
```

You should now have a worksheet like the one in Figure 9.2.

■ SECTION 9
The basic design

	A	B	C	D	E	F	G	H	I
1	Budget – First Half Year				Figures in '000,s				
2									
3			Jan	Feb	March	April	May	June	Total
4	Sales A		10000						
5	Sales B		6000						
6	TOTAL IN		16000						
7									
8	EXPENSES								
9	Materials		4800						
10	Labour		4000						
11	Commission		800						
12	Overheads		4000						
13	Power		3500						
14									
15	TOTAL OUT		17100						
16									
17	Balance		-1100						
18									
19	Bank A/c	-10000	-11100						

Figure 9.2

At this stage you might well be wondering about the supposed productivity benefits of spreadsheets – this could all have been done much quicker on paper. However, things will soon look up.

■ SECTION 10
Editing

In the next section we will copy January's formulae and values to fill the other months – so check them first, and correct any mistakes.

Correcting an entry

If you spot an error as or just after you have typed it, erase back to the mistake with the [Backspace] key and retype. Don't try to move the entry line cursor with the arrow keys. In normal entry mode, an arrow keypress transfers the data into the sheet and moves the worksheet cursor.

To make a change early on in a long entry, you need Edit mode.

Edit mode

To switch into Edit mode while you are still typing the contents, simply press [F2]. If the data has already been entered into the sheet, move the worksheet cursor back to it and press [F2].

In Edit mode, the typing cursor can be moved along the entry line, and characters inserted, deleted or overwritten. These keys have special functions:

[Left]	Move one character to left
[Right]	Move one character to right
[Ctrl] [Left]	Move five characters to left
[Ctrl] [Right]	Move five characters to right
[Delete]	Erase character under the cursor
[Backspace]	Erase character to left of cursor

[Insert]   Toggle Insert / Overwrite modes

In *Insert* mode, anything you type is inserted into the line at the cursor position. In *Overwrite* mode, new characters replace the existing ones. *Insert* is the default.

Emptying cells

A wrong entry in a cell can always be overwritten, simply by moving the cursor to it and typing a new entry. Sometimes though, you will want to remove the contents completely and leave it blank.

To clear a single cell, move the cursor to it and press the [Delete] key. (Or the [Delete] button on the mouse palette.)

To clear a cluster of cells use the Edit I Erase command, as described in Section 7.

■ SECTION 11
Copying values and formulae

The Copy command

This powerful and invaluable command is found on the Edit menu. It can be used for copying single cells or blocks, and can create single or multiple copies. And the beauty of it is that when formulae are copied, their cell references are intelligently adjusted to suit the new positions. Let's put it to work, using the worksheet we developed in Section 9.

Sales A are a steady 10,000 each month. The value should be in C4 already. We'll copy it across the row. To do this we have to call up the command and tell it what to copy and where to write the copies. It is easiest if you start on the origin cell.

1 Move to C4.

2 From the **Edit** menu, select **Copy**. Quattro prompts for the source cells. It assumes that you want to copy a block of cells, starting at the current one:

```
Source block of cells: C4..C4
```

If you are on the right cell, just press [Return] to accept this. If not, press [Escape] and point to C4.

3 Now, where are the copies to go? The entry line prompts:

```
Destination for cells: C4
```

If you just wanted a single copy in D4, you would now point to that cell and press [Return]. As it happens, we want to copy the value right across the row. Point to the first cell

(D4), press [.] and point to the end of the block, to give the definition D4..H4.

4 Press [Return] to complete the command.

Now see what happens when a formula is copied. Call up the Edit I Copy command again, but this time make the source cell C6, and the destination block D6..H6.

The original formula in C6 was +C4+C5. When it is copied into D6 it becomes +D4+D5, and likewise across the row. Unless you tell it different, Quattro assumes that cell references are relative. That is, when you write +C4+C5 in cell C6, what you mean is 'add up the contents of the two cells above this one'. Copy the formula to another part of the sheet, and the cell references are automatically altered so that the formula continues to have the same meaning. By and large, this is what is wanted – it certainly is in this case.

(Quattro also has *absolute* references for those times when you want to keep a cell reference constant as the formula is copied. We'll look at these in Section 14.)

Block copying
The formulae and figures in the rest of column C are the same for the rest of the half-year apart from the lower Power costs in Spring. We can use a block copy to fill in the other five months in a single operation. Let's take it step by step.

1 Move to C9 – the top of the block to be copied.

■SECTION 11
Copying values and formulae

2 Pull down **Edit** and select **Copy**.

3 For the Source block, spread the highlight down to C19.

4 For the Destination, move to D9, press [.] and spread to H9.

5 Press [Return] to complete the command.

Note that you only need to give the top row of the destination. A copy of the C9..C19 contents will be dropped into each of the columns starting at row 9. If you preferred, you could give the destination block as D9..H19. It would still work exactly the same.

At this point you might like to enter the Sales B values for Feb to June, and the Power costs for April to June (Figure 11.1).

Finishing off
The sheet needs totals in Column I. A @SUM() function would do the job nicely:

```
I4: @SUM(C4..H4)
```

The simplest way of getting this into the other totals is to copy it right down the column. It will give you 0s in rows 7, 8, 14 and 16, where there is nothing to add. These can be easily be deleted out of the way.

This has given us a worksheet in which a budget could be planned. Let's take it one stage further, so that it can cope with actual

SECTION 11
Copying values and formulae

	A	B	C	D	E	F	G	H	I
1	Budget – First Half Year				Figures in '000,s				
2									
3			Jan	Feb	March	April	May	June	Total
4	Sales A		10000	10000	10000	10000	10000	10000	60000
5	Sales B		6000	8000	10000	12000	14000	16000	66000
6	TOTAL IN		16000	18000	20000	22000	24000	26000	126000
7									
8	EXPENSES								
9	Materials		4800	5400	6000	6600	7200	7800	37800
10	Labour		4000	4500	5000	5500	6000	6500	31500
11	Commission		800	900	1000	1100	1200	1300	6300
12	Overheads		4000	4000	4000	4000	4000	4000	
13	Power		3500	3500	3500	3000	3000	3000	19500
14									
15	TOTAL OUT		17100	18300	19500	20200	21400	22600	119100
16									
17	Balance		-1100	-300	500	1800	2600	3400	6900
18									
19	Bank A/c	-10000	-11100	-11400	-10900	-9100	-6500	-3100	24000

Figure 11.1

income and expenditure and variations from targets. There are several options, as always. We'll go for the most compact one as it introduces another key feature of the Edit menu.

First, all the figures must be entered for the planned budget. The totals in column I can then be copied into the next column *as values, not formulae.* This will fix them permanently.

Copying values

1 Move to I4, the start of the source block.

2 Pull down the Edit menu and select Values.

■ SECTION 11
Copying values and formulae

3   Stretch the highlight down to I14 to define the source block.

4   Give J4 as the destination and press [Return] to complete.

```
      A      B      C      D      E      F      G      H      I      J      K
 1  Budget - First Half Year
 2
 3                  Actual            |      Projected
 4           Jan    Feb    March  April  May    June   Actual Budget Diff
 5  Sales A   9500   9000   9400  10000  10000  10000   57900  60000  -2100
 6  Sales B   5000   6500   8600  12000  14000  16000   62100  66000  -3900
 7  TOTAL IN 14500  15500  18000  22000  24000  26000  120000 126000  -6000
 8
 9  EXPENSES
10  Materials 4600   4950   5700   6600   7200   7800   36850  37800   -950
11  Labour    4400   4600   4750   5500   6000   6500   31750  31500    250
12  Commission 725    775    900   1100   1200   1300    6000   6300   -300
13  Overheads 4200   5000   4050   4000   4000   4000   25250  24000   1250
14  Power     4000   4500   3500   3000   3000   3000   21000  19500   1500
15
16  TOTAL OUT 17925  19825  18900  20200  21400  22600  120850 119100  1750
17
18  Profit/Loss -3425 -4325  -900   1800   2600   3400    -850   6900  -7750
19
20  Bal.  -5000 -8425 -12750 -13650 -11850 -9250 -5850
```

Figure 11.2

The planned figures can now be overwritten with the actual figures, month by month, as they become available. The totals in column I will record the changes, while the planned totals in column J remain unchanged. To pick up the variation from the budget, write simple subtraction formulae in the adjacent cells:

        K4: J4 - I4   {Budget - Actual}

■ SECTION 11
Copying values and formulae

Before you go any further, save this worksheet to disk, then you can turn off the machine and knock off for the day without losing that hard work.

■ SECTION 12
Simple filing

The File menu handles the saving, loading and similar filing management jobs, as might be expected. It also handles those operations that are related to multiple worksheets. Let's ignore these for the time being and concentrate on saving and loading files.

Filenames

All data files must have a name which identifies them for the computer and, just as importantly, to you. The MS-DOS system insists that the filenames must follow certain rules. The name must:

■ Not have more than eight characters

■ Not have spaces between characters

■ Not use punctuation, apart from underscores

Numbers may be used freely, and MS-DOS doesn't distinguish between upper and lower case letters. MS-DOS also allows you to add a three-character extension to the name, but Quattro reserves these extensions for its own purposes. Quattro will tack . WQ1 onto all worksheet filenames to identify them as worksheet files. When you start to output sheets as text files – for later printing or for incorporation into a word-processed report – you will find that it tacks . PRN to the names of these files.

For your own purposes, a filename should make the nature of the worksheet as clear as possible. BUDGET is a perfectly good name – as long as you only have one budgeting file in your system. BUDGET91 would be a better way of identifying the 91/92 budget sheet and BDGMAY91 would make it clear that this was the version produced in May.

■ SECTION 12
Simple filing

The File List window

In several of the File operations a small window opens on the screen. It displays the *file specification* and the worksheet files present in the current directory. The file specification takes the form:

```
C:\QPRO\*.W??
```

The first part of this is the *path* – the drive letter, directory and sub-directory names that specify where to look for files. In the example, the path refers to the C: drive and the QPRO directory. The second part of the specification is almost always the same – `*.W??` – and uses the standard MS-DOS wildcards to find files of any name where the extension starts with 'W'. It therefore picks up any Quattro files (`*.WQ1`) and any produced by Lotus 1-2-3 (`*.WK?`).

A couple of other things to notice in the File List window. There is a highlight bar on the first of the filenames – use this to select files for loading. And there will usually be a prompt on the top line. This will vary with the operations.

Lastly, you may like to know that pressing [F3] at this point will toggle between the small File List window and a full-screen display. As you move the cursor over the files in the full display, the date and time of the last save and the size of the highlighted file are shown in the top line. This can be useful for tracking down files.

Saving worksheets

The procedure for saving depends on whether you are saving the sheet for the first time, resaving the sheet or saving with a new name.

■ SECTION 12
Simple filing

The first save

Quattro automatically gives a new sheet the temporary name SHEET1 – and SHEET2, SHEET3, . . . when using multiple sheets. But this is only to identify it while you are using it within the system. It must be given a proper filename for saving.

Follow this procedure when you are saving a file for the first time.

1 Pull down the **File** menu and select **Save**.

2 The File List window opens, with the prompt Enter save file name: (Figure 12.1). Ignore the highlight bar – unless you really want to overwrite an existing file.

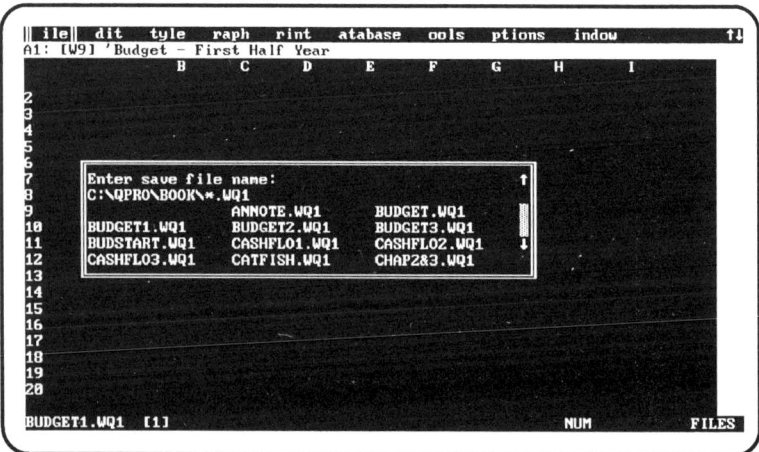

Figure 12.1

3 Press [Escape]. The file display disappears and a cursor appears, ready to take the filename.

4 Type the name and press [Return] to complete the save operation. You might notice that the worksheet's new name is displayed on the bottom line of the screen.

Saved again

Saving is simpler the next time around – although there is now the question of what to do with the old copy of the file.

1 Pull down the File menu and select Save.

2 A window opens with the message File already exists, and the options:

> Cancel
> Replace
> Backup

3 Select **Cancel** if the whole operation is a mistake – perhaps you should have saved the file with a different name?

4 Select **Replace** if you are sure the old copy is not wanted.

5 Select **Backup** if you want to play safe. The old copy will be renamed with .BAK in place of .WQ1. Should the new copy prove to be a mistake, you can still retrieve the original version (see below).

■SECTION 12
Simple filing

Saving new versions

Worksheets are often used as templates. The sheet that was designed to handle this year's budget will serve for next year's as well. A job-costing worksheet could be used to cost every job that comes in. It is only the data that changes – the basic structures remain the same. In these sort of situations, the trick is to create a 'blank' that contains all the calculations and relationships, but which has no actual numbers. This blank is then loaded at the start of a work session, data is added to it and then the completed sheet is saved under a new name.

The process is the same as for the first save, except that this time you select Save As from the File menu.

Retrieving files

The Retrieve option loads a file from disk to replace the current worksheet – if any. It is usually a simple process.

1 Select Retrieve from the File menu.

2 When the File List window opens, move the highlight bar to the relevant file and press [Return].

3 Wait a moment while it loads. (Very large files take several moments!)

Possible problems:

■ The file is not on the current disk or directory. The simplest solution here is probably to escape from the Retrieve operation, pull down the File menu again and select **Directory**. Edit or type in the new path to complete the command. All subsequent filing operations will then be to that directory.

■ The current sheet has been changed but not saved. A prompt box will appear asking you if you want to lose your changes. If you don't, select **No** to cancel the operation. You can then save the old sheet before retrieving the new one.

Clearing the sheet

You do not need to wipe the system clean before loading a new sheet – the Retrieve operation will do a wipe before pulling in the file, and it is possible to have several worksheets active at the same time (see below). Sometimes, though, you will want to clear the current sheet before starting to write a new one from scratch. It's simple and (almost) foolproof.

1 Pull down the File menu and select Erase.

2 If the current sheet has been changed but not saved, you will be asked to confirm that you want to lose the changes.

N.B. File I Erase only clears the sheet from the Quattro system. It does not affect the disk file.

Closing and opening files

The **File I Close** and **File I Open** options serve no real purpose while you are working with single sheets, but they are worth mentioning at this point. Multi-sheet working is covered in detail in Part 7.

File I Open allows you to load in a second (or subsequent) worksheet, while keeping the current ones active. The file selection process is exactly the same as Retrieve in other respects. Once

■ SECTION 12
Simple filing

the new file is loaded, you can switch between the active sheets by pressing [Shift]-[F6].

File I Close shuts down the current worksheet. It does not save it – so Save before a Close. If you close the only active worksheet, the grid display and all but one of the top menu labels disappear. The only menu then available is **File**, and even this has a reduced set. To get the system started again you must use either **File I Open** to retrieve a worksheet, or **File I New** to start a fresh one.

Leaving Quattro Pro
This is another simple, foolproof job. When you have finished, just select **File I Exit**. If the sheet needs saving, Quattro will offer a **Save and Exit** option.

■ SECTION 13
The flexible worksheet

While it is generally quickest to get your worksheet design right from the start, altering the structure of a sheet is not difficult. Rows and columns can be inserted or deleted, and blocks of cells can be moved, copied and erased. Sometimes it will be necessary to edit formulae after a restructuring, but if you tackle it the right way, you can often get Quattro to adjust the formulae automatically.

Insert and Delete
Insert moves existing rows down – or columns to the right – to make room for one or more new rows (or columns). Cell references in existing formulae are altered so that they continue to refer to the original cells, in their new positions. Delete is the exact opposite, removing rows or columns from the sheet. Formulae are adjusted, though any references to deleted cells are replaced by error messages.

The commands themselves are very straightforward to use. To insert a row:

1 Move the highlight bar to any cell on the row above which you want the new one to be inserted.

2 Pull down the **Edit** menu and select **Insert**.

3 Select either **Rows** or **Columns** from the prompt box.

4 If more than one new row is wanted, stretch the highlight bar down.

5 Press [Return] to complete the command.

Edit I Insert Column works the same, except that the highlight bar should start on a cell in the column to the right of the insert.

The two Edit I Delete options are directly equivalent.

Maintaining block references

Suppose you were recording the number of hours spent by various workers on a particular job. You might run up a worksheet something on the lines of Figure 13.1. The formula in B7 – @SUM(B3..B6) – is perfectly adequate for adding the four workers' hours. It is copied across into C7, to handle Week 2. Then a problem arises.

```
          A          B          C
 1   Job Hours
 2                Week 1    Week 2
 3   Bill             12         10
 4   Sandy            14         15
 5   Joe               6          5
 6   Sue               3          4
 7                    35         34
 8                @SUM(B3..B6)
 9
10   Hourly Rate      10
11   Labour Costs    350        340
```

Figure 13.1

Dick is brought into the team. A new row 7 is inserted into the sheet for his hours – but the formula must be adjusted, as it still only adds the cells in rows 3 to 6. Of course, it is no great sweat

■ SECTION 13
The flexible worksheet

to edit a single cell, but an Insert could equally well affect a whole string of formulae.

Here's the solution. Plan for Inserts whenever you write a block reference. Leave a blank line above and below the set of rows – or at both ends of a set of columns – and include those end cells in the block reference. In Figure 13.2, the total formula in B9 reads `@SUM(B3..B8)`. If we add a new worker, and insert a new row 8, the existing cell B8 will be pushed down to B9, and the block reference will likewise change to `(B3..B9)`.

```
           A          B          C
   1    Job Hours
   2              Week 1      Week 2
   3
   4    Bill           12         10
   5    Sandy          14         15
   6    Joe             6          5
   7    Sue             3          4
   8
   9                   35         34
  10              @SUM(B3..B8)
  11  Hourly Rate      10
  12  Labour Costs    350        340
```

Figure 13.2

The extended block technique is similarly useful when deleting. If you delete Bill's or Sue's row from Figure 13.1, you delete a cell that makes up part of the reference in the SUM formula. It will then change to `@SUM(ERR)` – not a lot of use. However, in Figure 13.2, you can delete the end rows from the data block, without ruining the formulae, because the references are to cells beyond these.

59

■ SECTION 13
The flexible worksheet

Moving parts

In an Edit|Move operation, the data and formulae in a block of cells are copied to another part of the sheet and the source block wiped clean. It is similar to an Edit|Copy followed by an Edit|Erase, but with a subtle difference in the way that cell references are handled.

Cell references *in* moved cells are not changed. Move @SUM(B3..B8) from column B to C, and it will still read @SUM(B3..B8). If it had been copied, the references would have been adjusted to `C3..C8`.

Cell reference *to* moved cells are changed. On the job costing sheet we might move the `Hourly Rate` date up to the top line. The command would be:

```
Edit|Move  A11..B11  to C1
```

The formula in B12 which had read +B10*B11, would be adjusted to +B10*D1.

```
           A         B         C         D
1    Job Hours           Hourly Rate    10
2              Week 1    Week 2
3
4    Bill            12        10
5    Sandy           14        15
6    Joe              6         5
7    Sue              3         4
8
9                    35        34
10             @SUM(B3..B8)
11
12  Labour Costs  350       340
```

Figure 13.3

60

■ SECTION 14
Absolute references and named blocks

Absolute and relative references

We noted earlier that references are normally *relative*. If you write +B4 into cell C4, Quattro treats this as meaning 'the next cell to the left'. This happens to be B4. If you copy the formula, the cell reference changes, but it continues to refer to the cell to the left of the one containing the formula.

If you want a reference to point to the same cell, when and wherever it is copied, the reference must be made *absolute*. For example, a worksheet like the one in Figure 14.1 could be used for salesmen's commission. The formulae to calculate commission, starting in C7, could be written in the form +B7*0.05. This will copy without any bother, but if the commission rate changes, it will be necessary to rewrite the formulae. It is more efficient to write the rate into a cell - B3 – and refer to that in the formulae. Should the rate change, a simple entry into one cell is all that is needed. However, there's a problem.

```
         A         B        C         D         E
1    Commission  on  Sales
2
3    Comm Rate     0.05
4
5    Staff       Sales     Commission
6
7    Smith       1250        62.5  +B7*$B$3
8    Jones       2300        115
9    Robinson    1750        87.5
10
```

Figure 14.1

If you copy the formula +B7*B3 down the column, both references adjust to the new positions, and the resulting formulae are useless. The solution is to make B3 into an absolute reference. To do this, press [F4] – the Absolute key – after the reference has been

■SECTION 14
Absolute references and named blocks

given. Dollar signs appear before both the letter and the number in the reference. Copy +B7*B3 down a cell, and it becomes +B8*B3.

There are variations on the full absolute. It is possible to fix either the row or the column alone, leaving the other part of the reference relative. Pressing [F4] toggles between the alternatives.

B3   Full absolute
$B3   Column absolute, row relative
B$3   Row absolute, column relative

In practice, almost all references will be either purely relative or absolute.

Names

Once a worksheet grows beyond a single screen, cell references start to become awkward to use. It is inconvenient to point to a reference in a distant part of the sheet, and rarely possible to remember references – especially if you have restructured the sheet and hence changed cell positions. Named cells and blocks provide a simple solution to these problems.

Once a name has been allocated to a block, that name can be used in any subsequent command or formula in place of the reference. Names are far easier to remember than references – as long as you use meaningful ones – and, if the sheet is restructured, the names continue to refer to the same relative cells.

Creating named blocks

The rules for block names are far freer than for worksheet names. In fact, the only real rule must be that the name is meaningful – and therefore easy to remember. It should also be shorter, rather than longer. SALES_WINCHESTER_JANUARY91 is very meaningful, but fraught with possibilities for typing errors. WINJAN91 will do the same job far easier.

1 Move to the cell, or a corner of the block, to be named.

2 Pull down the **Edit** menu and select **Names**.

3 From the Name sub-menu, select **Create**.

4 Type in the name at the prompt.

```
Enter name to create
```

5 Stretch the highlight area over the block and press [Return].

If the worksheet cursor was not on the right cell at the beginning, you can press [Escape] at step 5, to release the highlight bar and move it into place.

The routine changes slightly after the first name has been created. Next time round the prompt window displays a list of existing names, and the prompt reads:

```
Enter name to create/modify
```

To modify a block definition, pick its name from the list then carry on to the next stage.

Using names in formulae

Figure 14.2 shows a fragment of a worksheet in which names are being put to good use. It holds the sales data for three branches of a computer store. This simple example spreads well beyond the visible screen, and a fully developed sheet of this type could be extremely large.

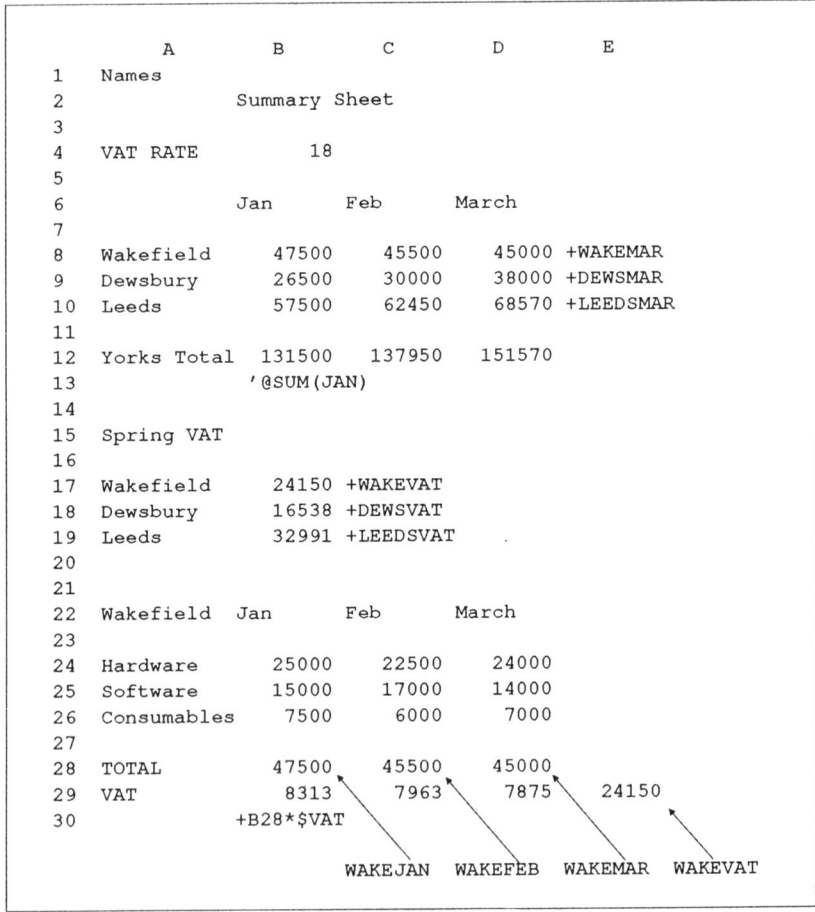

```
            A         B         C         D         E
 1   Names
 2             Summary Sheet
 3
 4   VAT RATE         18
 5
 6             Jan       Feb       March
 7
 8   Wakefield       47500     45500     45000 +WAKEMAR
 9   Dewsbury        26500     30000     38000 +DEWSMAR
10   Leeds           57500     62450     68570 +LEEDSMAR
11
12   Yorks Total  131500    137950    151570
13                 ' @SUM(JAN)
14
15   Spring VAT
16
17   Wakefield       24150 +WAKEVAT
18   Dewsbury        16538 +DEWSVAT
19   Leeds           32991 +LEEDSVAT        .
20
21
22   Wakefield  Jan       Feb       March
23
24   Hardware        25000     22500     24000
25   Software        15000     17000     14000
26   Consumables      7500      6000      7000
27
28   TOTAL           47500     45500     45000
29   VAT              8313      7963      7875     24150
30                 +B28*$VAT

            WAKEJAN   WAKEFEB   WAKEMAR   WAKEVAT
```

Figure 14.2

Absolute references and named blocks

Names are used in several ways here. The VAT rate is written into the top of the sheet, and its cell (B4) named as VAT. When the VAT amount is calculated in B29, for instance, the formula reads:

    +B28*$VAT

You will see that an absolute reference is used to allow the formula to be copied across to other months.

Each of the monthly totals for each shop is also named. For example, the January total in Wakefield is named as WAKEJAN. When the worksheet's designer gets round to writing the summary part of the sheet, it is much simpler to type +WAKEJAN into B8 than to try to get the cell reference. It is worth noting that as the name is left in its relative form, it can be conveniently copied here. Copy +WAKEJAN from B8 to C8..D8, and the formulae +WAKEFEB and +WAKEMAR appear in those cells, in just the same way that B28 would have been changed to C28 and D28.

Names have also been used in the total calculations. The block B7..B11, for example, has been named JAN. It can then be added by the formula @SUM(JAN). There's little immediate benefit from this – it would have been quicker to omit the naming process and use direct references – but it may be useful should the designer want to do further work on the January figures, elsewhere on the sheet.

Other Name options
Edit I Name Delete removes a name and its definition. Just pick the name from the displayed list and confirm that you mean it.

Edit I Name Labels can be handy when you want to name a whole batch of cells at once. It allows you to use existing labels as names – but it only works where there are labels adjacent to the cells to be named. The labels can be to the Right, Down, Left or Up from the data cells – but must be immediately next to them.

In Figure 14.2, you could label the January totals for the three shops (in B8..B10) as WAKEFIELD, DEWSBURY, LEEDS by the sequence: ,

1 Select **Edit I Name Labels**.

2 Select **Right**.

3 Define the block as A8..B10 – including both labels and the cells to be named.

Edit I Name Reset deletes all names in a single operation.

Edit I Name Make Table writes onto the sheet – at a chosen spot – an alphabetical list of the names, with their blocks alongside. This is useful for reference, particularly after an absence.

PART THREE

Presentation on screen and paper

■ SECTION 15
Basic styling

Spreadsheets are more than number-crunchers – Quattro Pro more so than most. They are means of presenting data to make it more meaningful. Graphing is a key part of this, but equally important is the attractive layout and appearance of the worksheets themselves, on both screen and paper. It is not difficult to make the sheets look better, and it pays real dividends in making the information more accessible.

Whether or not you can make full use of Quattro's presentation facilities does depend, of course, on your hardware. Variable column widths, lines, boxes and the full range of number formats can be achieved on any screen and most printers, but variable row heights, alternative fonts, background shading and integral graphs require EGA/VGA screens.

It is important to remember that the way that data is displayed and the way it is held in memory are two different things. A number may be formatted to appear on screen as an integer, yet be held in memory to fifteen decimal places.

All the formats on the Style menu are applied at cell level and take up memory. For the most efficient use of space, change the default settings to suit the way that you will want most of your data to appear and set formats only where essential, and only on occupied cells.

The Style options
Most aspects of presentation are controlled from the Style menu. Some are so crucial to readability that their use should be almost automatic; others will only really come into play when you need a final polish to impress the boss, the clients or the bank manager. In this section, we will concentrate on the key ones.

Basic styling

Most of the Style options are managed in the same way. Once you have selected the option, Quattro will prompt for the block in which this option is to be set. It assumes that the block will start at the current cursor position, and is waiting for you to point to the other corner. If the cursor is not in a suitable place, press [Escape] to release it, and start again.

Widths and heights
Column Width may not be at the top of the menu, but it is often the first Style option to be set. This affects the width of the current column only. Type in the number of character spaces, or use the [Left] and [Right] arrow keys to pull the column to the desired size.

Reset Width restores the current column to the default width – normally 9, but adjustable via the Options menu (see Section 50).

Hide Column allows you to fold the sheet vertically, completely removing a column from view. Useful for tucking confidential calculations out of sight! To get back to the cells, in order to view or edit them, call up the option again and select **Show** from the final sub-menu.

Block Size has four sub-options:

- ■ **Set Width** is the same as **Column Width** except that it works on a block of columns, not a single one; and **Reset Width** will restore blocks of columns to the default setting.

- ■ **Auto Width** is one of the new features of version 3.0, and can be a handy time-saver. It sets individually the widths of a block of columns according to the length of the longest item in each. Your only input here is to specify how many character spaces are required between the columns.

■ SECTION 15
Basic styling

■ **Row Height** is only applicable to EGA/VGA screens running in WYSIWYG mode, and would be used where different font sizes have been set (see Section 17). The height is given in points, with a default of 16.

Alignment

The Alignment option is used for both labels and numbers. The default settings are for labels to be aligned to the left and numbers to the right, which is fine much of the time. However, where labels are acting as headings for columns of figures, Right or Centre alignment will make for a closer link between heading and figures. Index and reference numbers often look better left aligned. Any values which are to be added together should remain right aligned – and be formatted consistently so that the decimal places line up down the column.

Default Styles	Aligned and Formatted
Totals	Totals
1234.5	1234.50
12.34	12.34
123	123.00
1.23456	1.23

Numeric format

Numbers are stored with 14-digit accuracy – the 15th digit being used to round the one before. In practice it means that when the bill exceeds £999 trillion you forget about the pence!

Several of the formats allow you to set the number of decimal places. The default is 2, but you can set it for anything between 0 and 15 decimals.

Where a number is too long to fit into the cell width in its given format, Quattro displays a row of asterisks (*********) to show this. Change the format for a more compact one, or widen the column.

Negative numbers are shown with a prefixed –, except in the Currency and Thousands separator (,) formats. These display negative values in brackets, following the common accountancy convention.

General is the default format. In this, numbers are displayed as they were entered – as long as the column is wide enough. If there are too many digits, then the number will be shown in the more compact Scientific format.

Fixed displays values with a given number of decimal places, but with no other punctuation. Overlong fractions are rounded to the nearest digit, and short ones packed out with 0s. It is probably most useful where you want to show values as integers (Fixed 0 d.p.), or as money (Fixed 2 d.p.); for example:

```
     Value        Fixed 0 d.p.     Fixed 2 d.p.
    1.23456            1               1.23
    123.4             123             123.40
    0.012              0               0.01
  1234567.8         1234568        1234567.80
```

Scientific or Exponential notation divides the values into digits and powers of ten. The digit part is always a value between 1 and 10, i.e. with the decimal point after the first figure. Multiply this by the power of 10 given after the **E** to get the true value. For example:

```
1.234E+02 = 1.234 x 10^2  = 1.234 x 100  = 123.4
3.456E-01 = 3.456 x 10^-1 = 3.456 x 1/10 = 0.3456
```

The number of digits displayed is set by you, but also depends upon the width of the cell. If you set 10 decimal places, 123,456,789.123 would still appear as 1.23E+08 in a 9-wide cell, but would be 1.234567891E+08 in a 16-wide cell.

Currency gives the fully-fledged money appearance, with an adjustable number of decimal places, commas as thousands separators and a dollar sign at the start. This can be changed to a £ or other currency symbol via the Options menu (see Section 50, *Setting Options*). Negative values are shown in brackets. This format makes numbers significantly longer – 1234 (4 characters) becomes $1,234.00 (9 characters) so be prepared to widen columns when using it.

Thousands separator (,) is effectively the same as Currency, but without the symbol.

```
        A         B         C         D         E         F
 1   Formats              Column Width 9
 2
 3
 4   General   Fixed 0   Sci 2     Currency Thous ,   Percent
 5
 6   0.123457         0 1.23E-01     £0.12     0.12    12.35%
 7   1234.56       1235 1.23E+03 ********1,234.56 ********
 8        123       123 1.23E+02   £123.00   123.00 12300.00%
 9       -123      -123 -1.2E+02  (£123.00) (123.00)********
10  -1234.56      -1235 -1.2E+03 *************************
11  12345678   12345678 1.23E+07 *************************
12  1.23E+12   ********1.23E+12 *************************
13
14
```

Figure 15.1

■ SECTION 15
Basic styling

Percent multiplies values by 100 and adds a % sign at the end. 0.15 would thus appear as 15%, assuming 0 decimal places.

+/- produces crude bar charts – with rows of +'s or -'s according to the value of positive or negative numbers. I suspect it is only included for compatibility with early versions of Lotus 1-2-3, as I have yet to find a use for this format.

Text displays formulae as text rather than as their resulting values. Useful during debugging.

Hidden blanks out the display in cells. Like the Hide Column option, this is useful for tidying away intermediate calculations or secreting confidential data.

Reset restores the numeric format to the default setting.

■ SECTION 16
Dates and time

Dates can be typed in as simple text. '20th April 1991 is a perfectly valid label, but this makes very poor use of the available facilities. For Quattro, a date should be more than just a label for a day, it should be something with which to calculate. It can tell you how many days have passed between two dates and what the date will be in so many days from now or from any given day. This is all managed by treating dates as the number of days which have elapsed since the start of time. Philosophers will no doubt disagree as to when this was, but as far as Quattro is concerned, time started on the 31st December 1899 and – Nostradamus take note – it ends on the 31st December 2099.

Entering dates
This always present something of a problem. How do you tell a spreadsheet that '27/3' means the 27th of March and not a division sum? The Quattro solution is ingenious, quicker to use than that of the main competitors – when you have got used to it – but a bit fiddly.

1 Press [Ctrl]-[D]. The word DATE pops up into the bottom status line.

2 Type the date in the format day/month/year. Miss out the year and the current one is assumed, and only bother to give two digits unless you want to specify a year in the next century. The 20th April 1991 could be entered as 20/4 or 20/04/91 or 20/4/1991. All work.

You must give a valid date in the correct format – Quattro is unforgiving. Type 30/2 and it will give you 15 as an answer; type 4/20 and you'll get 0.25.

When a date is accepted by the system it is converted to a date value – the number of days that have elapsed since the start of time. Type in 5/4/91, for instance, and though 05/04/91 will be displayed on screen, if you look at the cell contents you will find that they read 33333.

For reasons best known to Quattro's programmers, you cannot edit dates successfully unless you have set a Date format for the cell. Try to edit an unformatted date, and it will turn back into a simple number – you meant the 6th, not the 5th April so you change the entry to 33334, and that's what is then displayed. Set a Date format, and you can change the date value to your heart's content, without losing it as a date!

Date formats
These are accessed via the Numeric Formats in the Style menu. There are five alternative, falling into two groups. In all cases, the day number is shown with a leading 0 if it is a single digit; likewise the months, where appropriate. Year numbers are only shown as two digits unless they are in the next century.

Menu Choice	Display Style
DD-MMM-YY	05-Oct-91
DD-MMM	05-Oct
MMM-YY	Oct-91
Long International	05/10/91
Short International	05/10

If desired, the display order can be changed to the Month-Day format. This is managed through the Options menu (see Section 50).

Today's date
This could have been easier! There is a function – @**TODAY** – which reads the system's clock. Unfortunately, it converts the date to a Quattro date value and displays that on screen. You must then set a Date style for the cell to be able to read it properly.

■ SECTION 16
Dates and time

As it is a function, working in real time, it is updated every time the sheet is recalculated. This can be very useful. On a sheet designed to manage credit sales, you would record the date of each invoice. The age of the debt can then be found easily be using @TODAY. In Figure 16.1, the formula in H11 reads @TODAY - F11, and when this sheet was examined on the 4th April, the debt was seen to be 34 days old. Time to send out a reminder!

If you want to capture today's date, and fix it permanently for future reference, copy the cell onto itself using the Edit I Value command. Or type it in directly – that may be quicker.

```
      ...        F          G           H
      ...
      10        Date    Amount Due   Age of Debt
      11       01-Mar     £235.00        34
      ...
```

Figure 16.1

Time
The system's clock holds the time as well as the date, and this too can be read by a function. However, like @TODAY, it needs a bit of processing to be really useful.

@NOW returns a decimal value, where the whole number part is the day number and the fraction is the time since midnight. To get a meaningful result, select the **Time** option of the Date sub-menu and pick a format from the choices available. It is basically a question of whether or not you want seconds, and whether or not you use a 24-hour clock.

Time Options	Display Styles
HH:MM:SS AM/PM	10:35:43 PM
HH:MM AM/PM	10:35 PM
Long International	22:35:43
Short International	22:35

■SECTION 17
Desktop spreadsheeting

The desktop publishing concept has been a mixed blessing. While it has enabled many people to present their ideas more effectively – and more cheaply – than ever before, it has also been responsible for excesses that no self-respecting typesetter would ever have allowed into the printshop.

For the most part, the sensible use of column widths, alignment and numeric formats is all that is required in a worksheet. Further enhancement serves its purpose in items produced for public consumption – invoices, reports, catalogues and the like – but should be used sparingly. Lines and boxes will keep sets of figures together, or apart; the limited use of shading or of different font styles and sizes can make key items stand out, but if over-used serves only to confuse.

These decorative effects should only be applied when the work-sheet's layout has been finalised. Any Insert, Delete or Move operations that affect enhanced areas of the sheet are quite likely to chop off bits of lines and boxes or leave gaps in the middle of blocks.

Lines and boxes
The **Line Drawing** option on the Style menu allows you to draw lines within or on any or all sides of a block. Though the lines take up space on screen, they fit between rows and columns, rather than occupying cells. It is therefore not necessary to leave room for lines when planning the worksheet's layout.

To add lines:

1 Move to the top left corner of the box to be enhanced.

■ SECTION 17
Desktop spreadsheeting

2 Pull down the Style menu and select Line Drawing.

3 Spread the highlight area over the block to define it.

4 From the Placement menu select one of:

All	Outside and Inside
Outside	Top, Bottom, Left & Right
Top	Above the block only
Bottom	Below only
Left	To the left only
Right	To the right only
Inside	Horizontal and Vertical
Horizontal	Between the rows within the block
Vertical	Between the columns of the block
Quit	

5 From the Line Type menu select one of:

None	To remove unwanted lines
Single	
Double	
Thick	

6 The routine returns to the Placement menu. Repeat steps 4 and 5 or Quit.

Shading
With fewer options, this is simpler than Line Drawing:

■ SECTION 17
Desktop spreadsheeting

1 Move to the top left corner of the block.

2 From the Style menu select Shading.

3 Select None (to remove existing shades), Black or Grey.

4 Define the block.

Fonts

Quattro has eight different fonts available from its menus at any one time. The default fonts are all Bitstream Swiss or Dutch, from 8 to 72 points in size, in black ink and for the most part plain, with a single Italic. As long as one of these will do the job, setting fonts is as simple as adding shade.

1 Move to the top left corner of the block.

2 From the Style menu select Font.

3 Select the font by number, 1 to 8.

4 Define the block.

Editing fonts

Tucked at the bottom of the **Style I Font** menu are three options: **Edit Font**, **Reset** and **Update**. These allow you to assign your own definitions to the eight Font styles, reset them to the system defaults, and store new definitions as the defaults. For each one you can set the Typeface, Point Size, Style and Color. Explore the possibilities – the combinations are almost endless. But be prepared for a wait when you want to print the file (or for the screen to refresh on a WYSISWYG display), as any new fonts will have to be created beforehand.

■ SECTION 18
Printouts

Printing out from Quattro is simple and satisfying – as long as your printer can deliver the goods. This should rarely be a problem. What is so impressive about Quattro is not so much the quality of the laser printouts, but what it can achieve with even the humblest dot-matrix printer.

At the quickest, it need take no more than a few seconds to set up the first print from a worksheet, and subsequent reprints can be produced with three keystrokes. If headings are required, they can be added easily enough, and fully formatted screen previews are available, whether you have a WYSIWYG system or not.

Of course, before you can get a printout, you need something worth printing. The Budget worksheet developed earlier could be used, but you might like to run up a new sheet that makes use of some Style options, both to explore those and to test out the capabilities of your printer. The following Invoice worksheet (Figure 18.1) will do the job.

The Invoice template
This sheet is designed to be used as a 'template' – a blank to be re-used time and again as the basis for actual working sheets. When an invoice is needed, the template is retrieved, sales details added and the invoice printed out. If a file copy is wanted, the revised sheet is saved under a different name.

The formulae on this sheet are few and simple. Assuming the same layout as Figure 18.1, they would be:

Net = Per Unit * Qty
```
E19:  +C19 * D19
```

Edit I Copy down to E30.

81

INVOICE PREPARATION

> (Your Name)
> (Address 1)
> (Address 2)
> (Address 3)
>
> VAT No..........

INVOICE To:

(Name)	Date
(Address 1)	Invoice No.
(Address 2)	Your Ref.
(Address 3)	

Ref.No.	Item	Per Unit	Qty	Net
A23/011	Leather Widgets, Small	4.75	12	57.00
A45/258	Assorted Gizmos	3.50	10	35.00
C78/123	Combination Gadgets, with chain	15.95	6	95.70
				0.00
				0.00
				0.00
				0.00
				0.00
				0.00
				0.00
				0.00
				0.00
				0.00
		NET AMOUNT		187.70
		VAT		32.85
		TOTAL		220.55

TERMS

....

....

....

Figure 18.1

Net Amount = total of all Net values
```
E32:  @SUM(E18:E31)
```

VAT = 17.5% of Net Amount
```
E33:  +E32 * 0.175
```

TOTAL = Net Amount + VAT
```
E34:  +E32 + E33
```

Use **Style I Numeric Format** to set the display style for those columns, C and E, that will contain money values. **Fixed** will probably be most appropriate, with **Currency** for the totals. In both cases, 2 decimal places would be the norm.

The Net formulae will generate zero values in empty rows. These unwanted '0.00' values can be hidden by setting the default style:

1 Pull down the **Options** menu.

2 Select **Formats**.

3 Select **Hide Zeros – Yes**.

4 Quit from the menus.

To get a suitable layout, use **Style I Column Width** to expand the item details column to around 30 characters. Column D, which will only hold integer quantities, could be reduced to 5 or 6 wide. Columns C and E may need to be widened if the sums involved are very large, or if they are to be displayed to more than 2 decimal places.

There are a fair number of lines in the design, but it only takes half a dozen operations to get them all in place. The **Outside** option will create the boxes around the firm's and the customer's details. For the main body, A18..E31, a combination of **Outside** and **Vertical** will create almost all the necessary lines – just add a line **Beneath** the headings. Complete the drawing with a box **Outside** the Net Amount and VAT, and a line **Beneath** the Total.

You may also want to add Grey Shades behind one or more of the areas of the sheet – it might be a useful way of highlighting your Terms of trade.

Instant printing
If the printer is ready, and you don't want any special print effects, getting a printout is simple.

1 Pull down the **Print** menu.

2 Select **Block** and point or type the cell references for the block to be printed.

3 If necessary, select **Adjust Printer** and use either **Skip Line** or **Form Feed** to get the paper to the right place.

4 Select **Spreadsheet Print**.

5 Select **Quit**.

The system uses the default settings for printer and layout, which are fine for quick draft copies for your own reference. Where the output is wanted for clients or others, it is worth spending a few moments to set those options that will give a more professional appearance.

Setting options

Options only have to be set once. They remain current while the sheet is in memory and are saved when the sheet is saved to disk. This can be a great time-saver. With templates, like this invoice sheet, the block definition and all the printer settings can be stored with the sheet. When an invoice has been made out, it can then be printed by the simple sequence /PS (Print | Spreadsheet Print) – three keystrokes!

Destination

By default this is to the First printer, and draft quality only. Select this option and you will see that there are five possible destinations for your output:

■ **Printer** (Draft Mode) – with an option to redirect to a second printer, if present. Fonts and shades are ignored, and lines are printed as characters.

■ **File** – either for later printing or for incorporation in a word-processed document. The file will be a simple ASCII text file, with all graphic effects ignored. Give the directory path, if different, and a filename. The system will automatically add a .PRN extension to the name, to identify it as a printer file.

■ **Binary File** – including all graphic effects, to be stored on disk for later output to a laser printer.

■SECTION 18
Printouts

■ **Graphics Printer** – which can be the same as the Draft printer, providing this can support graphics. The difference is in how the sheet is sent for printing. You must select this if you want anything other than plain character printing.

■ **Screen Preview** – select this if you want to check the appearance before committing the sheet to paper. The preview does not occur at this point, but when you give the Spreadsheet Print command. A **Zoom** option within the Preview allows you to check the details of appearance.

If Screen Preview is selected, you must reselect **Graphics Printer** for the output.

Layout
None of the Layout options are relevant to printing the Invoice, but they are worth noting for future reference.

Header and **Footer** allow you to specify a line of text to be printed at the top or bottom of each page – particularly useful for identification on a multi-page printout.

Break Pages calls for a form feed at the end of each page. The default is **Yes**, which is essential for single sheet work and generally the best way to use continuous stationery.

Percent Scaling only applies to final quality printing on a graphics printer. It can produce an enlargement of up to 1000% (10x), and reduce to the infinitesimal – though anything less than 70% is difficult to read.

Dimensions are by default given in **Lines/Characters**, but can be based on **Inches** or **Centimetres** if wanted.

■ SECTION 18
Printouts

Margins allows you to reset the top, bottom and side margins. The presence of the **Print to Fit** option (see below) means that you rarely need to bother with margin details. An exception would be when switching between wide carriage and standard paper.

Orientation is by default **Portrait** – the normal way up. For sideways printing select **Landscape**, or **Banner** for an unbroken sideways print on continuous stationery.

Setup String permits you to send control codes to the printer – in Draft mode only. The codes are given as three digit numbers, prefixed by a backslash; e.g. character 14, which turns condensed mode on for most printers, would be written \014. In practice you will rarely need to bother with these, as the other options, used with the Graphics printer, give far easier control over printed output.

Reset puts all the optional settings back to their default values.

Update stores the current settings as defaults.

Values gives a display of the current optional settings.

Quit exits from the Layout menu, to the main Print menu.

Other options
Headings would be used where you had a large table that spread over several pages. It allows you to take the column or row headings at the start of the table and repeat them on each page to identify the lines in the table. It should not be confused with the **Headers** on the Layout menu, which add a single line of text to the top of each page.

■ SECTION 18
Printouts

Format can generally be left to the default of **As Displayed**, though the **Formulae** option here may be useful when debugging a worksheet – it produces a list of cells and their formulae.

Copies – how many do you want?

Print to Fit is something I find to be less useful than first appears. Where the width of the printing block is such that it would spread beyond a single page width, the Print to Fit option will squeeze it into a page. This is managed by reducing the widths of the columns – which means that longer entries are chopped short. If a block is too wide for the page, use the Landscape Orientation, or reduce it evenly with Percentage Scaling.

PART FOUR

Simple graphs

■SECTION 19
Graphing essentials

Quattro's graphing facilities mirror the rest of the system. On the one hand, you can whip up very adequate, albeit spartan, graphs in a matter of moments; on the other, if you choose to spend the time and effort, you can produce fully enhanced, embellished and annotated charts. And as with 'desktop spreadsheeting', many people will find that the main problem will be knowing when to stop adding to the design.

Before you can produce any graphs at all, of course, you need a table of figures. The examples in this section are built around the data shown in Figure 19.1. This shows the last five years' sales figures for a firm and its market-leading rival. You may prefer to use a different – but similarly arranged – set of data.

	A	B	C	D	E	F
1	Simple Graphs					
2						
3		1987	1988	1989	1990	1991
4	No 1 Rival	250000	265000	280000	290000	295000
5	Our Co	15000	35000	87500	120000	155000
6						

Figure 19.1

Fast Graphs

Quattro has a *Fast Graph* facility which will convert a table of figures into a graph. Ideal for producing instant visual displays, it will also serve as a convenient starting point for more complex graphs. The keystroke sequence could hardly be easier or shorter:

1 Move to the corner of the data block – in this case B4. Press [Ctrl]-[G], or select **Graph I Fast Graph**.

2 Point to the opposite corner of the data block, or type in the cell references – here they would be B4..F5.

3 Press [F10] or select **Graph | View** to get a screen display.

4 Press any key to return to the worksheet.

The resulting graph should look like the one in Figure 19.2. There are three points to note here. First, the data block has been intelligently split into two series – our firm's and the rival's. Second, the values in the Y-axis have been automatically scaled to **thousands**. If they had been bigger, they would have been scaled to **millions**. This is also good news – it improves the appearance of the display by making the Y-axis easier to read. Last, but by no means least, the system has selected a Stacked Bar graph. This is not an appropriate display style for this particular set of figures. A simple line or bar graph would have been better here – and I suspect this is true in many cases. (After

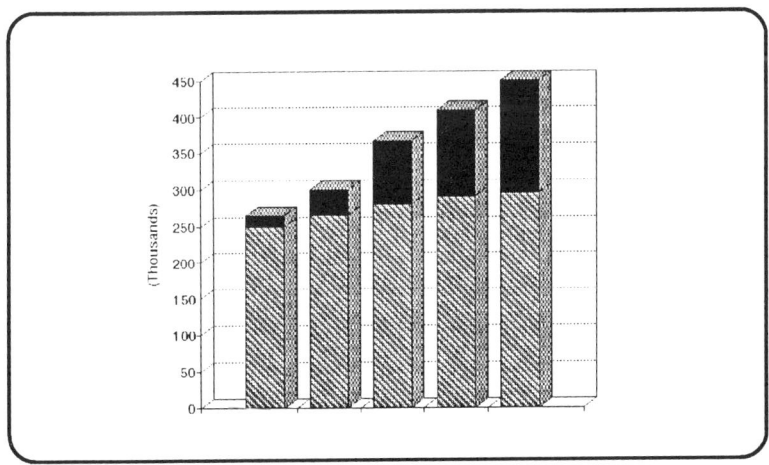

Figure 19.2

■SECTION 19
Graphing essentials

we have looked at graph types, you may wish to select something other than the Stacked Bar as the default – this is easily done.)

Selections from the Graph menu

While some menus close down as soon as you have made your selections from them, the Graph menu stays active until you choose to Quit or press [Escape]. This makes sense, for you will generally want to set a number of different options to create the final image. Another handy feature of the graphing system is that you can press [F10] at any point to view the graph, and when you return to the main screen, the display of menus will be exactly the same as when you left it. This makes it very easy to check and correct the options as you set them.

There's a choice between fourteen alternative **Graph Types**, and we will look at these the next section. Try a few now – you'll probably agree that in this case a Bar will give the best display.

A **Series** is any line – row or column – of data. The 1 to 6 Series headings refer to the sets of figures to be plotted on the graph. (6 is a sensible limit. Once you get beyond this, it becomes increasingly difficult to make sense of the image.) Nothing needs doing here, except to note that the first two series have been defined for you as part of the **Fast Graph** routine.

The **X-Axis Series** refers to the set of words or values that will label the horizontal axis. In this example, this will be the year numbers and they would be brought into the graph by defining the block B3..F3 for this series.

The **Text** sub-menu handles all other headings and legends on the graph. To get to the display shown in Figure 19.3, you would need to dip into the menu a couple of times.

92

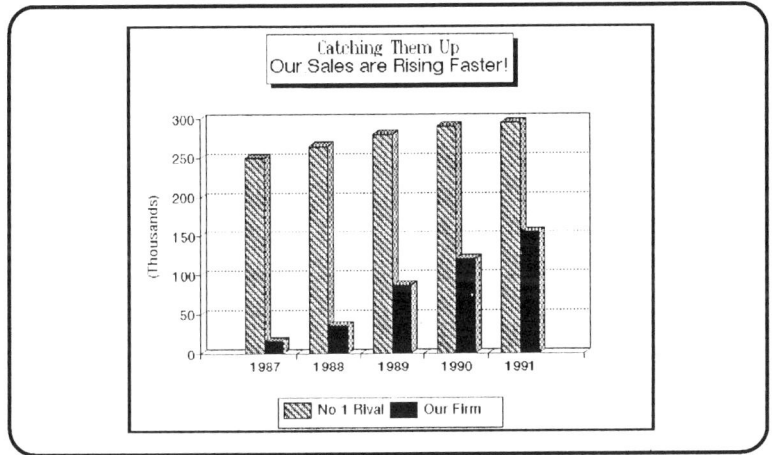

Figure 19.3

1st line is the first line of headings at the top of the graph. Select the option and type in whatever text is needed. Add a **2nd line** as a sub-heading, if you like.

Legends identify the series, and each one must be typed in individually. Here we need to add a suitable legend for the 1st and 2nd Series.

The **Fonts** used for each item of text can be altered – by type, point size or style – though you may well find that the default set are fine for most purposes. The styles and sizes have been well chosen to give a varied but well-balanced display.

If you have keyed in the example data and tried out the graphs, save the worksheet now – the graph settings will be saved with the sheet – as we will use this again in Section 22.

■ SECTION 20
Multiple graphs

A worksheet may be the basis of any number of graphs – either alternative views of the same data, or drawn from different data blocks. Individual graphs are identified by names, but before we turn to those, let's look first at how to change the data upon which these multiple graphs are to be based.

Resetting and redefining the data

To *clear all current settings* – data, labels and all else – select **Graph I Customize Series I Reset I Graph**. (You would have thought that they could have included a *New* option!)

To *delete a series* – but keep headings and other options, select **Graph I Customize Series I Reset**. Pick the series to remove it from the graph.

To *redefine a data or X-Axis series* – but leaving all other settings intact – select **Graph I Series**. Pick the series then point to or type the new references.

Identifying graphs by name

Once a graph has been given a name, it is saved and can be recalled for display and editing, and even linked into a slide show. These options are controlled from the **Name** sub-menu.

Select **Create** to save the current graph under a given name. These names follow the same rules as block names – essentially keep them brief and meaningful. The system expects you to create the name after you have finished defining the graph, and does not normally save later alterations. The working assumption here is that if you want to keep the revised graph, you will do so under a new name. This can be changed. If you set the **Autosave Edits** option to **Yes**, alterations to the current graph are automatically saved.

SECTION 20
Multiple graphs

The status of Autosave Edits has a crucial impact on the way in which new graphs are made and saved.

With **Autosave Edits No**:

1 Reset or redefine the data block and set options as desired.

2 Select **Name | Create** to save it.

3 If later alterations are made, select **Name | Create** again and pick the current name from the displayed list.

4 Return to step 1 if a further graph is required.

With **Autosave Edits Yes**:

1 Select **Name | Create** to start a new graph.

2 Reset or redefine the data block and set options as desired.

3 Return to step 1 if a further graph is required.

To bring back a named graph select **Display**, and pick out its name from the displayed list. (If you don't actually want to see the graph, hard luck. There's no other way to make a named graph current!)

■ SECTION 20
Multiple graphs

Quick slideshows

Whether you want to create a presentation for others, or a visual summary of key trends and comparisons for your own reference, it is much simpler to set up a 'slideshow' than to recall graphs individually. This will display on screen any given sequence of graphs, with each remaining in view until any key – or the mouse button – is pressed (see Section 48).

■ SECTION 21
Choosing the right type

Quattro offers fourteen different types of graph – rather more if you include 2-D and 3-D alternatives and the possibility of mixing types. What are they all for? In this section we will look at the key graph types. The examples will all be based on the tables shown in the worksheet in Figure 21.1. The first two both use the same data block – the Sales for Jan-June (B4..G6). Define the block using the **Fast Graph** method, then select the **Graph Type**.

	A	B	C	D	E	F	G
1	Sales & Expenses						
2							
3		Jan	Feb	March	April	May	June
4	Widgets	3000	4500	5000	7000	6500	7500
5	Gadgets	5000	5000	5000	5000	5000	5000
6	Gimbles	2000	2250	2000	1750	1000	800
7							
8	SALES	10000	11750	12000	13750	12500	13300
9	Expenses	500	675	650	700	600	650

Figure 21.1

Line graphs
Line graphs are good for showing trends. It is far easier to see the shape and slope of a line than to work out the relationship between figures in a table, or even between the varying heights of bars in a bar chart (Figure 21.2). Here it is quite clear that Widgets are forging upwards, Gimbles are on the way out and Gadgets are amazingly steady sellers.

Area graphs
These give a cumulative view of a table of figures. The first series is plotted as if on a Line graph, though the area beneath is shaded. With the second and later series, the values are added to the existing total at each position on the X-axis (Figure 21.3). Used with sets of sales figures, as here, the resulting display allows you

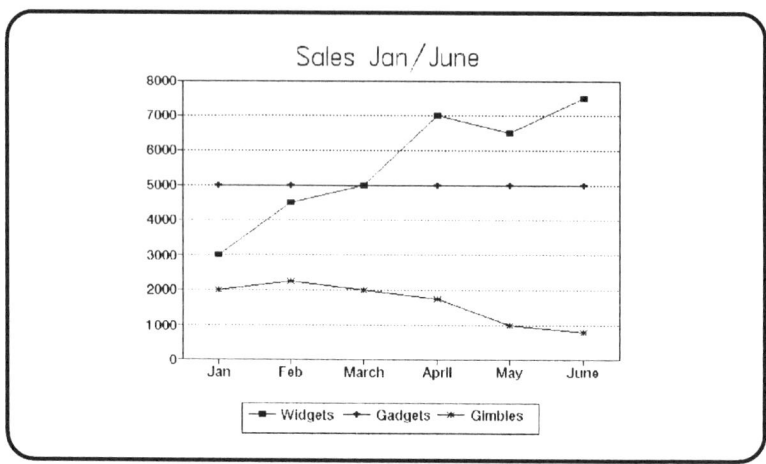

Figure 21.2

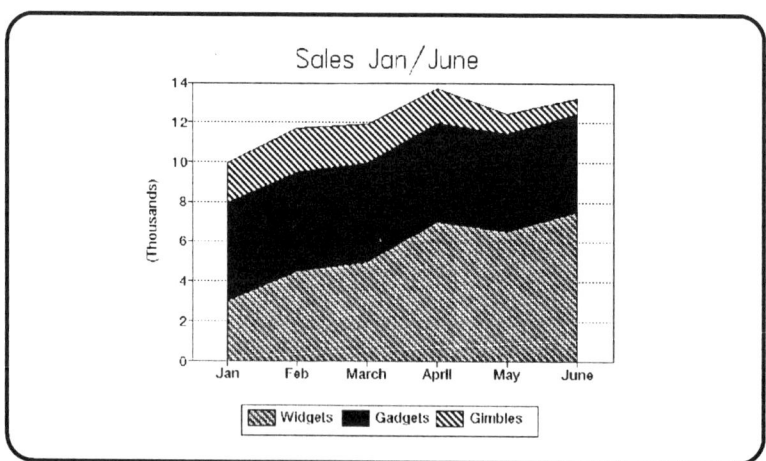

Figure 21.3

to see the overall trend of sales and the comparative contribution of each item.

Stacked Bar charts

In much the same way, the **Stacked Bar** is the cumulative equivalent of the standard bar chart. The trends are less easy to see, without the continuous lines joining each series of points, though the changes in comparative contributions may be more obvious – it is simpler to measure the heights of rectangular strips than of those bounded by sloping lines.

Rotated Bar

In most cases, I find these far less satisfactory than the standard upright bar charts. This is probably because we are trained to read left to right across a page, or to follow a table from the top down, while rotated bar charts must usually be read from the bottom upwards. This is certainly so where the X-axis is a time line and dates rise up the left-hand side.

The main exception is where the chart is the basis for a more decorated diagram, and the rotated bars can conveniently carry text or graphics from left to right. (See Section 47, on the use of the Annotator for enhancing graphs.)

XY graph

Use these to find the relationship – if any – between two sets of figures. In the Sales example, we would like to know if there is a correlation between Sales and Expenses. (As the figures are so simple, the correlation is fairly obvious anyway, but in real life you are less likely to have nice round numbers to work with!)

On an XY graph, one set of data forms the basis of the X-axis – here it is the Sales totals (Figure 21.4). Note that it is only a basis. The figures in B8..G8 are not used as markers along the X-axis,

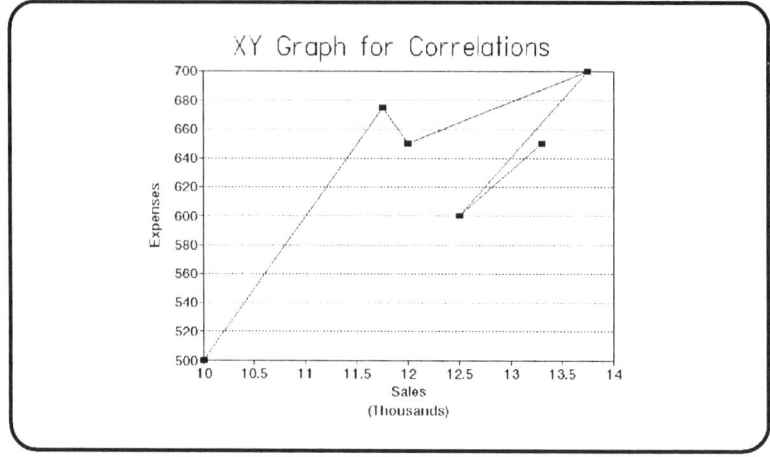

Figure 21.4

but its scale is calculated from the range of values in the block. The second set of data, here B9..G9, is then defined as the **1st Series**. The Y-axis scale is calculated, as normal, from this series. When the points are plotted, their horizontal position depends upon the value in the corresponding slot in the X-axis series.

If there is a fixed correlation between the values in the two series, the resulting line will rise diagonally across the graph. If there is an inverse correlation – i.e. one value rises as the other falls – then the line will run diagonally downwards. In the example, though the line is something of a zig-zag, most of the points are on the same diagonal, showing a fairly strong correlation between Sales and Expenses.

Pie and Column charts

Pie charts are an excellent way of showing the relative importance of the components of a whole. These might be categories of expenditure, contributions to gross profits by department or, as

100

■ SECTION 21
Choosing the right type

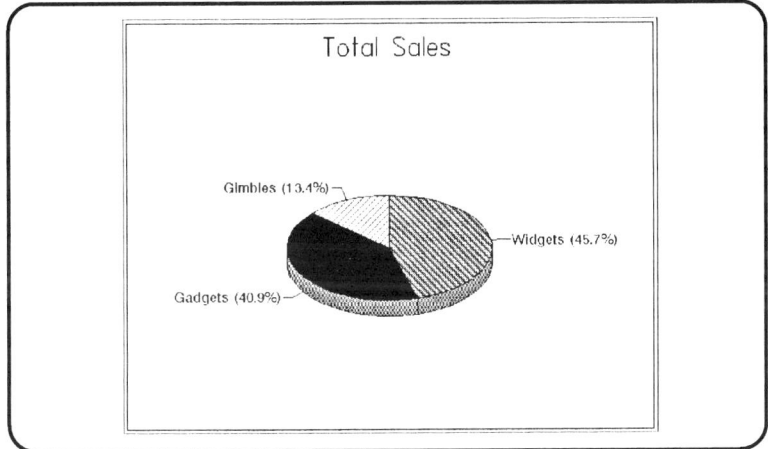

Figure 21.5

here, the breakdown of sales by product type (Figure 21.5). The main limitation of the Quattro pies (and one shared by most spreadsheets) is that they can only handle one series. It is simply not possible to get two or three pies on a single chart. As you will see in Section 23, you can insert several separate pie charts into a worksheet to get multiple displays or printout, but it is not the same as an integrated graph.

A second point to note about these displays is that all pies are basically the same size. This doesn't matter much with single displays, but can obscure the differences between overall totals when used in multiple displays.

Pie chart definition follows a different pattern to that of most other graphs. The data to be charted must be defined as the **1st Series**. The items are allocated to segments in the same order as in the worksheet, starting at the 12 o'clock position and working round clockwise from there. Each segment is, by default, labelled with its value as a percentage. This can be changed to an actual value via the Customize Series menu (see Section 22).

If you wish to add text labels, these must be defined as the **X-Axis Series**. **Legends** have no place here, though other titles can be added as usual.

Column graphs

These are a cross between pie and stacked bar charts. Like a pie chart they can only handle one series at a time, and their options and labels are set in the same way as pies. Their display however, is like that of the stacked bar, with values represented as rectangular blocks, piled on top of each other (Figure 21.6). It doesn't give the sense of wholeness produced by the circle of the pie chart, but the narrow vertical display could work well if inserted into a worksheet or accompanied by text in an Annotated design.

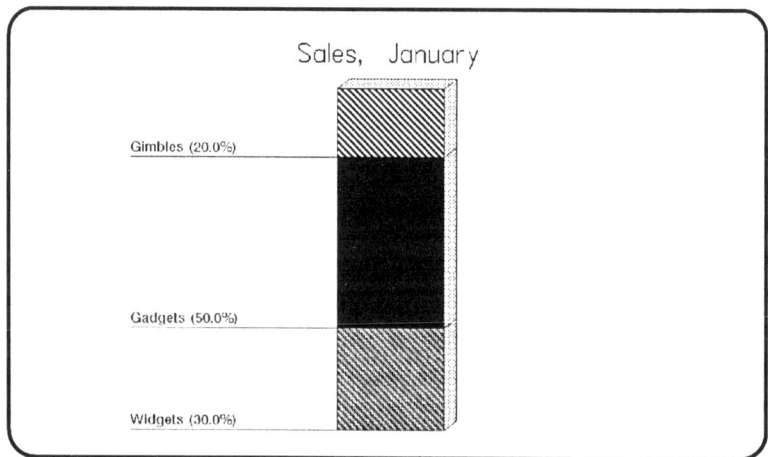

Figure 21.6

SECTION 21
Choosing the right type

Hi-Lo

The Hi-Lo graphs are ideally suited for displaying the range and movement of share prices or exchange rates. To use them, the highest values must be defined as the **1st Series** and the lowest as the **2nd Series**. These will then be plotted as the top and bottom points of a set of vertical lines. If other series are given, they will be plotted on those lines. If labels are required for the lines, define them as the **X-Axis Series**.

	A	B	C	D
		High	Low	Current
1	Hi-Lo Graphs			
2				
3	Share Prices			
4		High	Low	Current
5	BT	375	269	370
6	Rolls-Roy	179	139	163
7	Amstrad	93	60	71
8	IBM	72.7	55.6	60.25
9	GEC	222	166	200

Figure 21.7

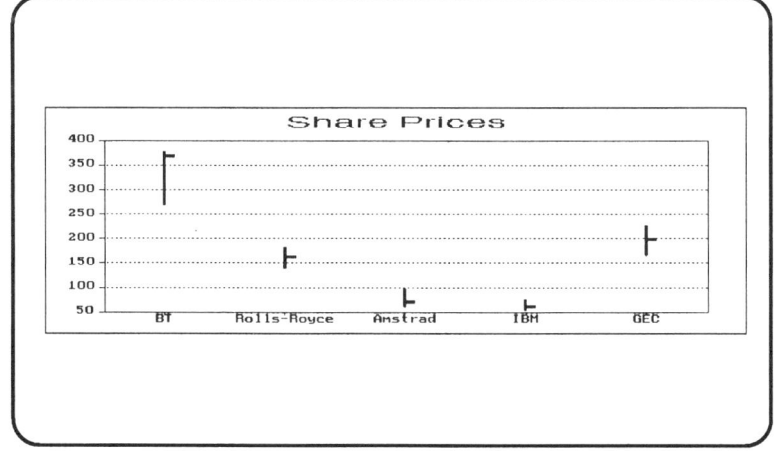

Figure 21.8

103

Figures 21.7 and 21.8 show the worksheet fragment containing the High, Low and Current prices of a group of shares, and the Hi-Lo graph produced from them.

3-D graphs
The normal Bar, Stacked Bar, Pie and Column graphs are usually displayed with a 3-D effect. The images are drawn to give an illusion of depth, but are arranged along the same baseline, side by side. The four types grouped under **3-D Graphs** go a stage further than this and plot the series in a three-dimensional grid, with the 1st Series at the back.

3-D graphs are not always a wise choice. If the values in the earlier series are lower than those in the later ones, their images may be totally obscured by the higher bars or blocks at the front. (Compare Figures 21.9 and 21.10 below.)

Defining the series, adding text and setting options are all performed in exactly the same way for 3-D graphs as for their 2-D equivalents.

Bar graphs are all but identical to 2-D bar charts, though displaying the series behind one another, rather than intermingled, does give more continuity to each set of values.

Step graphs are a variation on Bar graphs, with the individual columns widened so that they form a solid set of steps (Figure 21.9). As a result, lower values in rearward series are totally lost behind higher and nearer steps. At least in Bar charts the lower values can peek out between the nearer bars.

Ribbon graphs are the 3-D equivalent of lines, with each line converted to a flat ribbon snaking across the display (Figure 21.10). I rarely find this type satisfactory. If the ribbons cross more

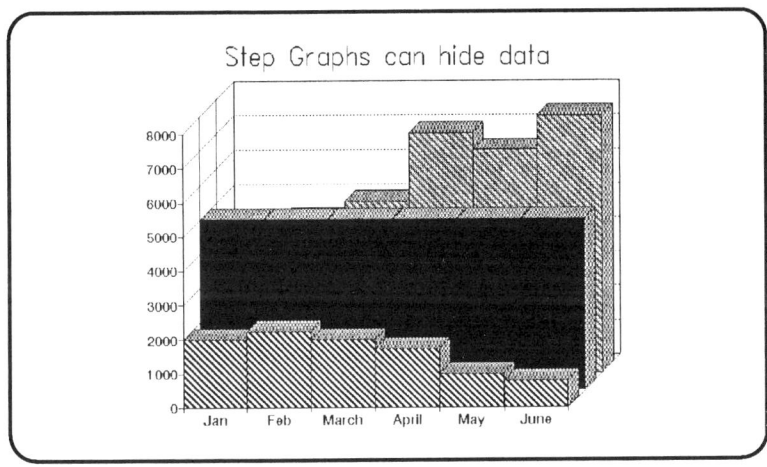

Figure 21.9

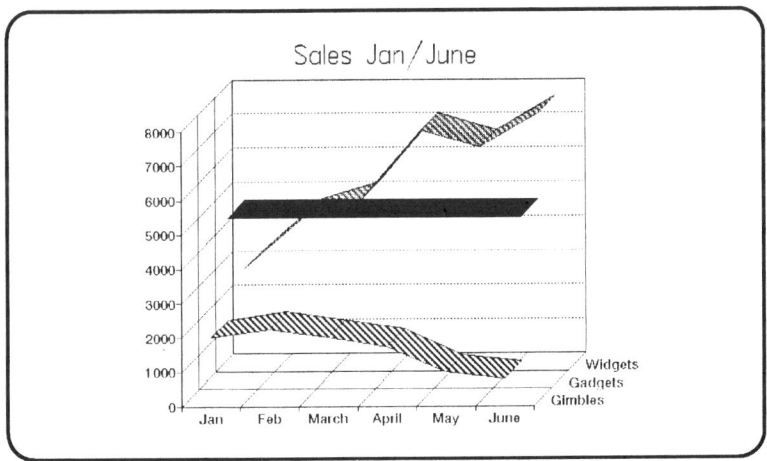

Figure 21.10

than once, they can start to look tangled, and comparative height is always difficult to see. With a solid block, the right-hand side carries the eye up from the base to give a sense of height and of distance from the front. Without this upright, the ribbons float and there is no immediate sense of which is in front or which is higher. This is especially the case where the values are all fairly similar.

3-D Area graphs are quite different from 2-D Area graphs. Instead, they are a development of the Ribbons display – and one which meets my complaints! In these, the area beneath each ribbon is filled to give a series of solid blocks, and height and depth are both much easier to see (Figure 21.11). Of course, the solid images produce the same problem, as with the Step graphs, that the forward series can obscure the values behind them.

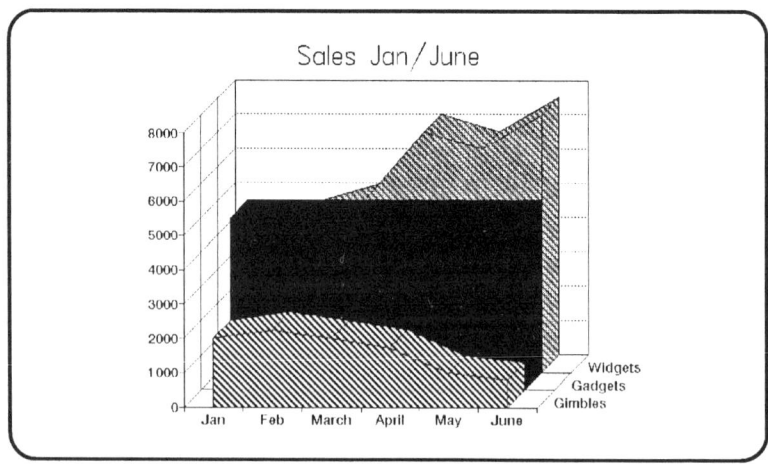

Figure 21.11

■SECTION 22
Customising the graph

We have already dipped into the **Customize Series** menu earlier, to find the **Reset** option. Why it is located in that menu still eludes me, for the other options are all of a distinctly different type. They are there to allow you to tweak and tailor the final display in a variety of ways.

Colors, **Fill Patterns**, **Lines & Markers** and **Bar Widths** are 'tweaking' options. Their impact on the appearance of graphs is marginal. A heavier line, a bolder colour, a more dense fill pattern can help to bring out a series, but won't change the essential nature of the display. All of these are options with which to experiment – and that's simply done. Change a setting, press [F10] to see how it looks, and change it again. You will stay at the same point in the menu while viewing your handiwork, so there's no time lost in working through sequences of keystrokes.

The remaining options have a more dramatic impact, and must be taken individually. To demonstrate them, we will use the worksheet given in Section 19, where the sales for Our Firm and those of our No 1 Rival were compared. One of the things that I hope will come out from this example, is that graphs do not necessarily help to bring out the meaning of a set of figures. If carefully designed, they can be thoroughly misleading – as most advertisers and politicians are aware.

Override Type
This option allows you to produce mixed bar and line graphs. The basic graph type must be either **Bar** or **Line**, but each series can then be set individually to either style. Define the same data into two series, and you can have a set of bars with a line joining their tops. With different data for each series, the alternative display type can emphasise the difference. In this case, we will set the 1st Series (No 1 Rival) as Bars, and Our Firm's sales as a Line.

■ SECTION 22
Customising the graph

Y-Axis

By default, all series are scaled against the left-hand Y-axis, the common scaling allowing a proper comparison to be made between the values. Sometimes this is not what is wanted. Suppose you were comparing the Sales and Expenses given in the example in the last section. The values in these series are so different that if you plotted them against the same scale, the Expenses would bump along the bottom, almost as a straight line.

Select a **Secondary** Y-axis for a series, and it is plotted against a new scale on the right-hand side of the graph. Like the **Primary** (left-hand) Y-axis, this will be scaled to encompass the full range of the values in the series that use it. As a result, the high value sales and low value expenses will both be displayed as lines or bars that use the full height of the grid.

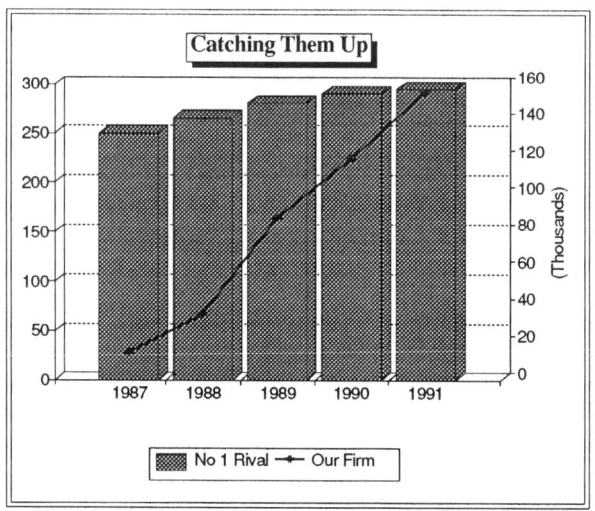

Figure 22.1

Customising the graph

Set a **Secondary** Y-axis for Our Firm's sales and see what that does to the display. We appear to have caught up the No 1 Rival! The use of the dual Y-axis also exaggerates the year-on-year increases in our sales and plays down the rival's growth (Figure 22.1).

Customising pie and column graphs
Pie graphs have their own set of options, to meet their special needs. Column graphs, which are essentially a variation on pies, can also be customised from this sub-menu.

The **Pies | Label Format** sets the style for the numeric values to be displayed beside the segments. By default, this is a figure showing its percentage contribution to the whole. It can be replaced by the actual **Value**, either plain or in $ money format; or removed altogether by selecting **None**.

Tick Marks – lines joining the label to the segment – are normally present, but can be removed. They are scarcely necessary unless there are a lot of segments, or several close together.

The **Explode** option allows you to emphasis one or more of the segments, by pulling them out of the main display. This is the only one of the pie options that does not also work with column graphs.

As with other graph types, you can achieve more subtle changes of emphasis, by careful choice of **Patterns** or **Colors**. These are the same as the options on the mainstream menu, except that they fix the appearance of individual data items, rather than of a whole series.

Overall options
While the **Customize Series** menu affects the way that data is displayed within a graph, the **Overall** menu affects the layout and appearance of the graph as a whole.

■SECTION 22
Customising the graph

The **Grid** option draws horizontal and/or vertical lines – in a variety of styles and the full range of colors – behind the data displays. The default is horizontal dotted lines.

Using the **Outline** option, you can place boxes of various types around the legends, the title and the whole graph.

The **Background Color** refers to the grid and to the on-screen display only. Here, as with all the colour options, you may well find that once you change one colour, a whole series of changes are needed before you have a well-balanced display once more.

The **Color / Black & White** option is probably of most use with CGA/EGA monitors, where the monochrome screen gives a higher resolution display.

The **2-D or 3-D** option can be largely ignored. By default, the 3-D effect is turned on, so that bars and pies have a chunky look. Switch to 2-D and the images are flattened. The difference is marginal on the bar graphs, but more noticeable in pie charts where the pie becomes a full round circle. 3-D graphs displayed in 2-D are most odd – the bars are flat panels rising from a 3-D base, and the Ribbons become lines, stripped of any sense of depth. Leave the 3-D on!

Updating graph settings

There is an **Update** option on the Customize Series menu. Use it with care, if at all. This saves as the new defaults all the current Customize and Overall settings, some – many? – of which will only be appropriate to the graph being produced at the time. When you have been using Quattro for a while and it has become obvious that there are certain options which you regularly set, then it will be time to Update the system.

■ SECTION 23
Graph printing

Graphs are printed, like the worksheets themselves, from the **Print** menu and in many cases will require no more than a few keystrokes.

To print the current graph direct to paper:

1 Pull out the **Graph Print** sub-menu.

2 Check that the **Destination** is the **Graph Printer** – it normally will be.

3 Check that your printer is on-line.

4 Select **Go** and sit back. There may be a delay while Fonts are built, though the printing itself is reasonably fast as graphics outputs go.

Graph Print options
If you want to print a graph other than the current one, select **Name** and pick your graph from the list.

The **Destination** may be a **File** – for later output to your printer – or a **Screen Preview**. This latter is well worth using in the early days as it lets you see how the graph will appear, without wasting paper and without waiting for the printer to do its stuff.

The **Write Graph File** options give you further alternative destinations. The main graphics file formats are supported – **EPS** (Post-Script), **Slide EPS**, **PIC** (1-2-3 compatible) and **PCX** (PC Paintbrush).

The **Layout** options control the position and size of the graph on the paper. By default the graph will be printed upright across the page, taking the full width and approximately half the height. This gives much the same proportions as in the screen view. **Width** and **Height** can be set independently – the graph will be scaled to fit within the limits, not clipped short.

If a large image is wanted, the best bet is to print the graph sideways on the page by setting the **Orientation** option to **Landscape**. You can turn of the normal **4:3 Aspect Ratio** to produce a bigger image, but this will not always work. Though the graph is enlarged to use the full height of the page, the width-wise fit is not checked and you are liable to lose the left- and right-hand sides of the design.

Graphs within worksheets

One of Quattro's neatest presentation features is the way it allows you to insert graphs into the body of a worksheet. This works on-screen with high-resolution monitors, but whatever the screen display, it is always possible to print the graph within the sheet. To have the source figures, the visual image and a text commentary together on a sheet can give a very complete view of the matter in hand.

To insert a graph into a sheet:

1 Check that you have a suitable area of blank cells where the graph will fit. If necessary, insert some extra rows or columns to give enough room. (This is not actually essential. The contents of cells within the display area are not over-written, but merely obscured while the graph is present.)

2 Pull down the **Graph** menu.

■ SECTION 23
Graph printing

3   Select **Insert**, and pick a graph from the displayed list.

4   Point to or type the references of the graph space.

To print a sheet with an inserted graph, use the normal **Spreadsheet Print** command – but do check that the **Destination** is a **Graphics Printer**.

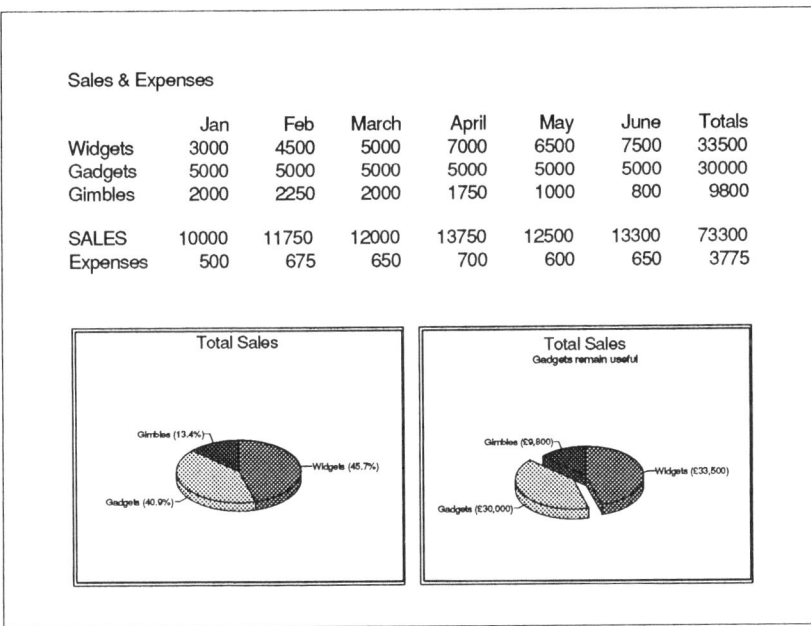

Figure 23.1

To remove a graph from a sheet:

1 If you can't remember the name of the graph, move the worksheet cursor onto its display area. The name will be shown in the entry line at the top of the screen whenever the cursor is on one of the area's cells.

2 Pull down the **Graph** menu.

3 Select **Hide** and pick the graph name from the list.

PART FIVE

The working spreadsheet

■ SECTION 24
Functional formulae

As a general rule, if you can express any relationship as a mathematical equation or as a logical statement, you can convert it to a Quattro Pro formula. Sometimes it will take a series of formulae rather than just one, at other times there will be a built-in function that will take away the need for complex formulae; but there will always be a way to get the maths into the worksheet. In this section we'll look at the simple mathematical relationships behind VAT, and the longer series of calculations needed for price setting.

VAT calculations
There are essentially two VAT calculations. The easy one is where you work out the VAT due on a given amount, and we did that back in Chapter 6. The more complex one is to find the VAT in a VAT-inclusive total.

HM Customs and Excise used to advise traders to use the **VAT fraction** of $3/23$. The equivalent one now is the even worse: $7/47$. Personally, I'd give this a wide berth and stick to a direct derivative of the percentage: VAT percent over 100 + VAT percent. Written as a maths expression, it would look like this:

$$VAT\ amount = (Total + VAT\ amount) \times \frac{VAT\%}{100+VAT\%}$$

You can test the formula by putting in some easy values. Suppose VAT were still only 15%, and you had an item costing £115.00, VAT inclusive. That would give us:

$$VAT\ amount = 115 \times \frac{15}{115}$$

The answer is clearly £15.00. The expression works. Translated into a worksheet formula, and with VAT as a decimal in a named cell this becomes: TOTAL * VAT / (1+VAT). For example:

SECTION 24
Functional formulae

```
        A            B
1
2   Inc. Cost    11.75
3   VAT           1.75  +B2*VAT/(1+VAT)
4   Ex. Cost     10.00  +B3-B2
```

Price setting

How much should a manufacturer charge for a new product to make a profit, or at least to break even? To get the answer we must look at the total costs and potential sales income. It's a mixture of the known and the estimated. There should be reliable figures for the fixed costs in designing and developing the product, and the unit manufacturing costs. Future sales can only be guessed at, but a good marketing department should be able to give reasonable estimates for possible sales at different price levels.

The Retail Price is one of the key variables in this worksheet. That is the one that the marketing people will be concerned with, and it is from this that we can calculate the Wholesale price. This can be established by calculating the Discount and subtracting it from the Retail Price:

> Discount = Retail * Discount%
> Wholesale = Retail – Discount

If you prefer, this can be run into a single formula:

> Wholesale = Retail – (Retail * Discount%)
> B5: +B3 - (B3 * B4)

A quick test with some simple values (£20.00 retail and 40% discount):

SECTION 24
Functional formulae

$$Wholesale \quad = 20 - (20 * 40\%)$$
$$= 20 - 8$$
$$= 12$$

When we start to fit the worksheet together, the Retail Price will go in the most accessible place (see Figure 24.1), as we will be writing a number of alternative values in here when using the sheet.

Fixed Costs will remain the same no matter what the sales. In the example in Figure 24.1, they have only three elements:

Fixed Costs = Development + Marketing + Other
```
B11: @SUM(B8..B10)
```

A more sophisticated model would include all the Fixed Costs incurred over the life of the product – the cost of investment capital for R & D and setting up the production lines, advertising, contribution to fixed overheads and the like.

The Variable Costs cover materials, labour and those overheads that are dependent upon production levels, and are generally expressed on a 'per unit' basis. In the real world, bulk purchasing and mass production are likely to create economies at certain levels. Here this has been ignored, and the equation has been simplified to:

Unit Cost = Labour + Materials
```
B16: +B14 + B15
```

The Unit Profit is also found by simple arithmetic:

Unit Profit = Wholesale Price – Unit Cost
```
B17: +B5 - B16
```

■ SECTION 24
Functional formulae

To find the Profit or Loss at any given level of sales, we calculate the total (per unit) profit and deduct the Fixed Costs.

Profit or Loss = (Sales * Unit Profit) – Fixed Costs

Now the level of Sales is the second key variable in this worksheet. We could treat it as we have Retail Price, and enter a succession of alternative values into a cell. We will, however, get a better overview of the situation if we generate a range of sales levels and calculate the profit or loss at each level.

	A	B	C	D	E
1	Price Setting		The Betta Mousetrap		
2					
3	PRICE			Sales	Profit/Loss
4	Retail	14.99		5,000	(12,280)
5	Discount	40.0%		10,000	(8,560)
6	Wholesale	8.99		15,000	(4,840)
7				20,000	(1,120)
8	FIXED COSTS			25,000	2,600
9	Development	10,000		30,000	6,320
10	Marketing	4,000		35,000	10,040
11	Other	2,000		40,000	13,760
12	TOTAL	16,000		45,000	17,480
13				50,000	21,200
14	VARIABLE COSTS			55,000	24,920
15	Labour	3.75		60,000	28,640
16	Materials	4.50		65,000	32,360
17	UNIT COST	8.25		70,000	36,080
18	UNIT PROFIT	0.74		75,000	39,800
19				80,000	43,520

Figure 24.1

Detour – lists of values

Quattro has a command, **Edit I Fill**, which will fill a block with a set of values. The **Start, Step** and **End** values are all optional, and the block to be filled can be a partial row or column or a 2-D block. That set of sales levels in Figure 24.1 could be created by the sequence:

119

■SECTION 24
Functional formulae

1 Pull down the Edit menu and select Fill.

2 Give 1000 for both the Start and the Step values.

3 Give 20,000 as the End value – it is more than can be reached, but that doesn't matter and the default of 8191 will cut the range off short.

4 Define the block to be filled as E3..E17.

This is a quick and easy way to produce a fixed set of values, but it is not the most convenient solution here. We will want to try alternative ranges of sales levels, but without having to go through the whole Edit I Fill process again. A better approach is to use formulae of the type:

Next value = Previous + Step

Here the first value in the range acts as the Start and Step value for the range. Note the use of the *absolute* reference in the formulae, so that it can be copied properly:

```
E4:  +E3 + $E$3
E5:  +E4 + $E$3
```

Enter 2,000 into E3, and the range becomes 2,000 to 30,000; enter 500, and the list goes up in 500s to 7,500.

The break-even point
One last formula, to find the Profit/Loss, will complete the sheet.

```
F3:  ($B$17 * E3) - $B$11
```

When this is copied down to F17, the references for Unit Profit (B17) and Fixed Costs (B11) will remain the same, while that for Sales (E3) will adjust to the new row numbers.

A glance down the Profit/Loss column shows clearly where the break-even point lies. (If you prefer the more visual approach, it takes only a moment to graph the figures. Use Fast Graph on the data in column F, and set the Type to Line.)

With a Retail Price of £19.99, the Betta Mousetrap will turn a profit on sales of a little under £4,500. The next question is, can the firm be sure of selling at least that many, at that price? It is time to look to the marketing department – and to bring their estimates into the calculations.

Probable profits
What we want from the marketing people are estimates of sales at different prices, and the likelihood of achieving those sales. Let's assume that they can come up with figures similar to those in the top half of Figure 24.2. These show, for instance, that with a retail price of £14.99, in the worst case the sales should reach 10,000, in the best case 50,000 and the most likely level is around 20,000. By entering the alternative retail prices and adjusting the range of sales values, we can get Profit/Loss figures for each sales level and price.

If you look at the summary projections in Figure 24.2, you will see that the 'Most Likely' sales level shows a profit only at the higher price of £19.99. This, then, would be the price that cautious managers should choose – or should they? A little probability analysis would help here. The 'Most Likely' is only one possible outcome, and the Worst and Best cases must also be brought into the calculations.

SECTION 24
Functional formulae

With sufficient market research, it should be possible to quantify the probabilities of each outcome. The Betta Mousetrap Co. is a bit limited in this direction, and the best they can do is estimate that the Most Likely outcome is twice as likely as either other case, at all price levels. Expressed in terms of percentage probabilities, this gives us the 25%, 50%, 25% values in the lower rows of Figure 24.2.

SALES & P/L	14.99		16.99		19.99	
Worst Case	10,000	(8,560)	4,000	(8,224)	2,000	(8,512)
Most Likely	20,000	(1,120)	8,000	(448)	4,500	848
Best Case	50,000	21,200	16,000	15,104	8,000	13,952
PROBABILITY						
Worst Case		25%	(2,140)	25%	(2,056)	25%	(2,128)
Most Likely		50%	(560)	50%	(224)	50%	424
Best Case		25%	5,300	25%	3,776	25%	3,488
			2,600		1,496		1,784

Figure 24.2

If we multiply the Profit/Loss value by the percentage probability for each outcome, it gives us a probable value. Thus, the Best Case profit at £19.99 is £13,952, but there is only a 25% probability of this; its probable value is 0.25 * £13,052 = £3,488. Add up the three probable values at each price and you get an overall probable value for that price. At the £14.99 price, this means that the 25% probability of a £21,200 profit more than balances out the (higher) probabilities of (lower) losses at the other sales levels.

The probable value approach works best where a firm has a number of product lines, as the losses on some will be offset by the gains on others. Where the main, or only, product is being priced, the firm would be better advised to go by the break-even analysis, for survival is more important than the chance of higher profits.

■ SECTION 25
Logic testing

Many calculations are conditional – a discount is only given if the total spent is above a certain level or if the customer has a favoured status, overtime is due if the employee has worked more than the standard hours. Performing these kind of calculations on paper, you have to stop and check the conditions before working out the discount, overtime or whatever, but with Quattro's logical capabilities such routine decision-making can be built into the worksheet.

The simplest form of logic test uses the relational operators to compare two values. Write this expression into a cell:

```
B5>100
```

It will display the value 1 if the test proves true – i.e. B5 is more than 100, or 0 if it is false (B5 is less than or equal to 100).

The other relational operators that can be used in this way are:

Operator	Meaning
>	is greater than
<	is less than
>=	is greater than or equal to
<=	is less than or equal to
<>	is not equal to

The tests work equally well on text, using the ASCII values of characters.

```
A10 >= "D"
```

This will display 1 if the string in A10 begins will "D" or any character than comes after it in the ASCII table.

■SECTION 25
Logic testing

Simple logic tests of this kind have limited value in worksheet calculations – there are better ways to handle things – but they are important in `Data Query` work (see Section 43).

IF...

The most useful of the logic functions is **@IF**. This tests a condition and allocates one of two values to the cell, depending upon the result. The basic form of the function is:

```
@IF(test, result-if-true, result-if-false)
```

In an invoicing worksheet, you might have a conditional discount. Expressed in words, this would read '*IF the total is more than £250, THEN the discount is 10%, ELSE the discount is 0%*'. Translated into a Quattro formula, to test the cell named TOTAL, the words THEN and ELSE are replaced by commas, to give:

```
@IF(TOTAL>250, 0.10, 0)
```

If the total was more than £250, this cell would have the value 0.10 for display and calculation purposes.

The values resulting from @IF functions do not have to be numeric. They may equally well be text labels, or other formulae or functions that produce either numbers or text. That last example could have been written:

```
@IF(TOTAL>250, 0.10, "Nil")
```

It would have had the same effect, as all labels have a zero value in calculations.

■ SECTION 25
Logic testing

Nested IFs

Where there are more than two alternative results, IF expressions can be written within each other. There might be three levels of discount. *IF the total is more than 250 THEN the discount is 10%, ELSE IF the total is more than 100 THEN the discount is 5%, ELSE the discount is 0%.* That translates to:

```
@IF(TOTAL>250, 0.10, @IF(TOTAL>100, 0.05, 0))
```

When writing IFs nested inside one another, check the commas and brackets carefully. In theory you can have a great many IFs in a single expression, but in practice it becomes too difficult to follow the logic – and therefore to spot errors – once you go beyond three. Here, as elsewhere, complex structures are best handled by breaking them down into smaller, more comprehensible components.

Multiple tests

Where a result is dependent upon two or more conditions, you can make use of the **#AND#** and **#OR#** operators. (Note that these do not start with the @ sign like functions, but are enclosed by hashes.) They can be used as stand-alone expressions:

```
B5>99 #AND# B5<=250
```

This would check that the value in B5 fell between 100 and 250. If both tests were true, the cell would display 1. If either test failed, the expression would result in a 0 value.

Multiple tests may also be used in IF formulae. Suppose that the firm gives a 10% discount if the customer is Trade or the bill comes to over £100. With customer type in the cell CUSTOMER, and the total in TOTAL, the expression would read:

```
@IF(CUSTOMER = "TRADE" #OR# TOTAL>100, 0.10, 0)
```

125

■ SECTION 25
Logic testing

How much tax?

We had a look at VAT in an earlier section, now let's turn to Income Tax, so that the Inland Revenue does not feel left out. The tax worksheet given here demonstrates the step-by-step approach to more complex calculations.

The sheet can be divided into two parts. The top is the data entry area. Your own figures for income and tax-deductible allowances go into column B, the current tax rates and threshold into the block E5..E7. For convenience, the cells should be named BASIC (E5), HIGHER (E6) and TOP (E7).

All calculations are performed in the bottom half of the sheet.

Total Tax Free (B10) is found by @SUM(B5..B9).

Taxable Income (B12, named TAXABLE) is a simple +B3 – B10. This must then be split into that which is taxable at the basic rate and at the higher rate.

Basic Band (B13, named ATBASIC) compares the taxable income with the threshold. If it is below the threshold, then it is all taxable at basic rate, otherwise only the amount up to the threshold should appear in this slot. The formula is:

```
@IF(TAXABLE<TOP,TAXABLE,TOP)
```

Higher Band (B14, named as OVERTOP) is very similar, but the resulting values here will be the amount over the threshold – if any – or zero. We could not simply use TAXABLE-THRESHOLD as that would produce negative values for lower earners.

```
@IF(TAXABLE>TOP,TAXABLE-TOP,0)
```

■ SECTION 25
Logic testing

The Basic and Higher Rate Tax formulae are straightforward multiplications of Rate by Band, and the Tax Due adds these together.

```
B16: ATBASIC*BASIC
B17: OVERTOP*HIGHER
B19: +B16+B17
```

```
                    A           B       C       D         E       F
 1    Income Tax
 2
 3    Annual Income         36000           Tax Rates
 4
 5    Personal Allowance    3295            Basic         0.25 BASIC
 6    Pension Contributions 1800            Higher         0.4 HIGHER
 7    Mortgage (non MIRAS)  3605            Threshold    23700 TOP
 8    Other Allowances
 9
10    Total Tax Free        8700
11
12    Taxable Income       27300 TAXABLE = +B3-B10
13    At Basic Rate        23700 ATBASIC = @IF(TAXABLETOP,TOP,TAXABL
14    Above Threshold       3600 OVERTOP = @IF(TAXABLETOP,TAXABLE-TO
15
16    Basic Rate            5925 ATBASIC*BASIC
17    Higher Rate           1440 OVERTOP*HIGHER
18
19    Tax Due               7365 = +B16+B17
20
```

Figure 25.1

If, in a future budget, the Chancellor decides to increase the number of tax bands, more formulae of the same kind can be added to split the taxable income and calculate each band's tax.

National Insurance can be calculated in a similar fashion, but is made more complex by the different classes of N.I. contributions.

■ SECTION 26
Lookup tables

Here's another way to get the worksheet to do routine chores for you. The Lookup functions allow you to write formulae that draw information from a table, for use elsewhere on the sheet. There are three related functions: **@VLOOKUP**, which draws from a vertical table; **@HLOOKUP**, which uses a horizontally arranged table; and **@INDEX** which picks the value from a block at a given row and column.

The basic concept is illustrated in Figure 26.1. The table of data is located at A10..C14. This is a vertical table, with the Reference Number, Item and Price in adjacent columns. (Those headings, by the way, are there purely for convenience, and not required by the functions.)

@VLOOKUP and @HLOOKUP

In any @VLOOKUP table, there must be reference numbers in the leftmost column, and they must be in numerical order if the lookup function is to work. In an @HLOOKUP table, that set of reference numbers is in the topmost row. The rest of the table is optional – as many columns or rows as you like, and containing whatever mix of labels and values you need.

To get data out of a @VLOOKUP table, you must give the reference number, the address of the block and the number of the relevant column. To get the latter, count the columns to the right of the reference numbers. In Figure 26.1, the Item data is in column 1, the Prices in column 2.

The formula in B4 reads:

```
@VLOOKUP(B3,A10..C13,1)
```

This takes the reference number from cell B3, checks down the leftmost column of the block A10..C13 to find a match, then copies

■ SECTION 26
Lookup tables

```
            A           B           C           D           E
1    Lookup Tables
2
3    Ref No.               12116
4    Item        5.25" QD Disks @VLOOKUP (B3,A9..C13,1)
5    Price                  7.99 @VLOOKUP (B3,A9..C13,2)
6
7                VLOOKUP  TABLE
8
9    Ref         Item            Price
10      12042 3.5" DD Disks       7.98
11      12043 3.5" HD Disks      18.49
12      12115 5.25" DD Disks      5.57
13      12116 5.25" QD Disks      7.99
14      12119 5.25" HD Disks      8.74
```

Figure 26.1

the data from the first column to the right. In the example, B3 holds 12116, which matches the value in A13, so the label 5.25" QD Disks is copied up into B4 by its formula. The Price is pulled into B5 by the similar formula:

```
@VLOOKUP (B3,A10..C13,2)
```

It is important to note that the matching operation is not an exact one. The Lookup functions use a <= (less-than-or-equal-to) test, and do so working down – or across – from the first cell. In the example, any value up to and including 12042 would pick out the data from the first line of the table. 12115 and 12116 will both reach Row 13. And any value higher than 12119 will drop off the end and produce an ERR message in the cell containing the formula.

The implications of this are two-fold. First, the reference numbers must be in the right order (see Section 45, on how to sort data into order); second, a non-existent number can still produce

SECTION 26
Lookup tables

results. For this reason, it is a good idea to build a cross-check into your Lookup operations. Even if you only want a price from the table, pull a description into view at the same time to check that it is the right item.

@INDEX

Though similar in effect to the @VLOOKUP and @HLOOKUP functions, @INDEX works in a rather different way. It does not use reference numbers, but relies instead on row and column numbers to identify the required data items. Its basic form is:

@INDEX(*table block, column, row*)

	A	B	C	D	E	F	G	H
1	Index Tables							
2								
3	Day No.		3	Wed	@INDEX(B8..G17,B3,0)			
4	Shift		5	13.00	@INDEX(B8..G17,0,B3)			
5	Duty Staff			Mark	@INDEX(B8..G17,B3,B4)			
6								
7				1	2	3	4	5
8		Time\Day	Mon	Tues	Wed	Thurs	Fri	
9	1	9.00	Jenny	Ali	Frances	Sally	Ali	
10	2	10.00	Ali	Mark	Frances	Dick	Julia	
11	3	11.00	Julia	Jenny	Bob	Jenny	Julia	
12	4	12.00	Frances	Jenny	Ali	Dick	Ali	
13	5	13.00	Dick	Bob	Mark	Frances	Bob	
14	6	14.00	Dick	Sally	Frances	Sally	Jenny	
15	7	15.00	Julia	Mark	Bob	Julia	Dick	
16	8	16.00	Mark	Jenny	Sally	Ali	Mark	
17	9	17.00	Dick	Bob	Julia	Sally	Jenny	
18								

Figure 26.2

■ SECTION 26
Lookup tables

The worksheet in Figure 26.2 manages a duty rota. The main table is in the block B8..G17, headed by the days of the week and the times of the day. The row and column numbers around the block are purely for reference and irrelevant to the operation of the function.

To get data out of the table, you must supply the column number – here it is the **Day** in B3 – and the row number – the **Shift** in B4. In the example, there are three INDEX formulae. The key one finds the name of the person on duty at the given day and time:

```
C5:  @INDEX(B8..G17,B3,B4)
```

In this case, the function looks into column 3 (Wed) and row 5 (13.00 hours) to find `Mark`.

The other two formulae are directed to the zero row and column to find the day name and time in hours, to provide a visual check that the correct index numbers were entered.

```
C3:  @INDEX(B8..G17,B3,0)
C4:  @INDEX(B8..G17,0,B4)
```

The last worksheet in this part of the book pulls together a number of the aspects of Quattro Pro that have been covered so far – the Style options, named blocks, @IF expressions, @VLOOKUP tables and printing. It is an invoicing utility, where the sheet takes care of all the calculations and much of the routine data entry. The example worksheet is for a fish wholesaler, which may be rather specialised, but the principles apply to all businesses. Work through the stages of its design and creation, adapting it as you go to suit your own line of trade.

The task is to produce printed invoices for customers, detailing the types, prices and quantities of fish that have been ordered, with the total costs to show carriage charges and bulk-purchase discounts. Carriage is charged at 25p per lb, and a discount of 10% is given to orders over £250. The types and current prices of fish are shown, with their reference numbers, in the table in Figure 27.1.

```
VLOOKUP TABLE

Code   Type                  Price
    1  Large Cod               £1.45
    2  Small Cod               £1.37
    3  Haddock                 £1.67
    4  Smoked Haddock          £2.30
    5  Coley                   £1.15
    6  Mackerel                £1.79
    7  Shrimps                 £3.90
    8  Lobster                 £4.65
    9  Crab                    £3.60
   10  Mussels                 £2.75
```

Figure 27.1

■ SECTION 27
Easy invoices

The top 30 rows of the worksheet are laid out in the style of the paper invoices that the firm used to use. It is here that data will be entered, and this is the part that will later be printed – twice – to give a copy for the customer and one for the files.

The sales clerk will only be required to enter the customer's details, date, invoice number, and then the reference number (column B) and quantity (column E) for each type of fish. @VLOOK-UP functions will pull the descriptions and prices into the invoice, and the calculations need no human intervention.

With worksheets of this sort, where the final appearance is important and where formulae are dependent upon data held in cells that are further on, it is often a problem knowing where to start. If you simply start at the top and work down, you can pretty well guarantee that your nice layout at the top will be ruined by column inserts, or width-setting, that you have to do later on. I prefer to start with the main working area, to help fix the overall layout, then add the data table and lastly the headers.

The Sales Details area
This is the key part of an invoice and the column widths required here must set the basic shape of the sheet. Leave room for our firm's and the customer's details, and enter the column headings across row 10.

Column A is left blank – by setting its width later, we can adjust the position of the invoice in the printed copy. (It's quicker to do that than to use the **Print I Layout Margins** command.)

The other columns should be headed Ref, Type, Unit Price, Quantity and Cost. The actual words are unimportant, but the order should remain the same. Widths should be set to suit the contents. How long is the longest description that will go into your

133

■ SECTION 27
Easy invoices

Type column? Are the prices so high, or shown to so many places of decimals that the standard 9-character width will be too small? At some point, either now or later, you should use **Style | Numeric Format** on those blocks that will contain Unit Prices and Costs, selecting either **Currency** or **Fixed, 2**.

We'll need some data before we can get much further.

The lookup table
This should be located away from the working area – either to the right or below. We'll leave 30 rows clear; if that isn't enough, more can be inserted afterwards. The table should follow the standard vertical pattern – the leftmost column contains the reference numbers, with descriptions and prices in the adjacent columns. In the example, there are only ten types of fish. Most firms will deal in rather more than that number of stock lines. However, at this stage of the worksheet design, you only need to enter enough to be able to test the lookup formulae that will draw on the table.

Use **Edit | Name Create** to name the table. I have called mine, unimaginatively, TABLE. When defining the block, extend it below the last data item to leave space for later additions.

Now back to the working area.

The formulae
An unadorned @VLOOKUP function will not do the job on a sheet where appearance matters, because if it cannot find a suitable reference number, it will display an intrusive error message. The solution is to wrap it up in an @IF. So, in the first row beneath the Type heading (here C11) you want a formulae like this:

```
C11:  @IF(B110,@VLOOKUP(B11,$TABLE,1),"")
```

134

INVOICE PREPARATION

TOWZER'S FISH SAL		To:
Dock Street		
Grimsby		
Tel: 0472 123456		

Date: Inv. No.

Code	Type	Unit Price	Qty	Cost
				£0.00
				£0.00
				£0.00
				£0.00
				£0.00
				£0.00
				£0.00
				£0.00
				£0.00
		Sub-total		£0.00
		Discount	0.00%	£0.00
			GOODS	£0.00
		Weight	0	
		Carriage @	0.26	£0.00
			TO PAY	£0.00

Figure 27.2

This only attempts to perform the lookup if a valid reference is present. If not, it displays an empty cell. Notice, by the way, the absolute reference for $TABLE, so that this remains unchanged when the formula is copied down the sheet. And take care with the commas and brackets on these multi-function formulae.

The Price is drawn from the data table in the same way:

```
D11:  @IF(B110,@VLOOKUP(B11,$TABLE,2),"")
```

Easy invoices

One more formula is needed to complete the row. The Cost is found by multiplying Quantity and Unit Price:

```
F11:  +E11*D11
```

Enter a suitable reference number into B11 and a quantity into D11 to test the formulae. If all is well, copy the three formulae down to row 22 – or wherever gives you sufficient room for the largest normal order.

The Sub-total is a straightforward SUM:

```
F23:  @SUM(F11..F22)
```

The label for this, as for the later summary calculations, can be written into whichever column looks best to you.

As the Discount is conditional upon the size of the order, an @IF statement is required to establish the percentage:

```
E24:  @IF(F23250,0.15,0) {F23 is the Sub-total}
```

The actual discount amount is then a simple multiplication:

```
F24:  +F23*E24 {Sub-total x Discount percentage}
```

Subtract the discount to get the GOODS cost:

```
F25:  +F23-F24
```

No VAT to worry about in the fish game, but there are carriage costs. First find the Weight by adding column E:

```
E26: @SUM(E12..E22)
```

The per lb Carriage charge is written into a cell (E27), for ease of alteration, then multiplied by the weight in the adjacent cell:

```
F27: +E26*E27 {Weight x carriage charge}
```

And we have the grand TO PAY total:

```
F28: +F25+F27 {GOODS + Carriage}
```

Enter a few more reference numbers and quantities to test that all the formulae work correctly, and check the various cell references if you get unexpected results.

Finishing off
First tidy up the working area. Column widths may need adjusting if you have labels in columns D and E, and you must check that the total width of the active columns will fit your printer.

The Cost formulae down column F will produce 0s on the blank lines. These look untidy. They can be removed by wrapping the multiplications in @IF functions, as we did with @VLOOKUP, but there is a simpler solution. You can set the sheet so that it does not display zero values, using the Options menu.

Hiding zeros

1 Pull down the **Options** menu.

2 Select **Formats**.

3 Select **Hide Zeros** and answer **Yes**.

4 **Quit** out of the menus.

Top and tail

Every business will have its own way of heading up invoices, and Quattro's **Style** options for Line, Shade and Fonts allow you a good deal of room for individuality. You may also wish to add a reminder of your terms of trade at the bottom of the invoice.

Hard copy

Pull down the **Print** menu and define the block to cover all the active part of the sheet. Check the appearance by a test print (Figure 27.2) or, if that is inconvenient, by redirecting the output to the screen.

When you are happy with its appearance, remove all the test data from the sheet and save it.

PART SIX

Finance and forecasting

■ SECTION 28
Loans and investments

Compound interest calculations used to be the bane of many an accountant's life. The choice was between interpolating from books of tables or struggling with complex equations – neither very attractive options. Spreadsheets have made life easier. Now, many calculations can be handled by ready-made functions, and for the rest it is only necessary to work through the equations once, building them into a sheet.

Mortgages and annuities

These are two sides of the same coin, the first being the repayment of a capital sum by regular outgoings, the other being a regular income purchased by a lump sum. In both cases there are four interdependent factors – the capital amount, the periodic payment, the interest rate and the number of payment periods. Given any three of these, the fourth can be found using one of Quattro Pro's financial functions.

There are two sets of almost identical compound interest functions. The first set dates back to earlier versions of Quattro and is retained for compatibility with this and with the widely-used Lotus 1-2-3 spreadsheet; the newer functions have optional extensions which improve their performance, but render them incompatible. We will focus on the latter.

These same abbreviations are used in all the functions:

Pv	Present Value of the capital sum
Pmt	The regular payment or repayment
Rate	Interest rate, expressed as a decimal, e.g. 0.10 or 10%
Nper	Number of periods – an integer value

■ SECTION 28
Loans and investments

Fv   Future value – the capital accruing or remaining

Type   An optional setting; 0 if payments are made at the end of each period, or 1 if made at the start. The default is 0.

Either the capital sums or the payments must be negative; the flow of money is two way. The interest rate and number of periods must use the same time frame; you cannot mix annual interest rates and monthly payments.

@PAYMT finds the repayments on a mortgage – or the annuity arising from a capital sum. Its basic shape is:

```
@PAYMT(Rate,Nper,Pv)
```

It also has the extended form:

```
@PAYMT(Rate,Nper,Pv,Fv,Type)
```

To find the annual repayment on a £50,000 mortgage over 25 years at 12%, you would use the formula:

```
@PAYMT(0.12,25,-50000)
```

This gives £6,375. Divide by 12 to get an approximation of the monthly repayment (£531.25). This won't be accurate as paying by the month reduces the capital and therefore the interest charges over each period. You will get a better result by expressing the rate and periods in terms of months, and if the repayment is made at the start of each month, the *Type* option should be set:

```
@PAYMT(0.12/12, 25*12, -50000)= £526.61
```

■ SECTION 28
Loans and investments

```
@PAYMT(0.12/12 = 5*12, -50000,0,1)= £521.40
```

Again, neither are exact as 12% p.a. is not the same as 1% p.m. – we'll return to this point shortly.

@PVAL calculates the Present Value – the capital sum that can be raised at a given interest rate, time and payment. It has the forms:

```
@PVAL(Rate,Nper,Pmt)
@PVAL(Rate,Nper,Pmt,Fv,Type)
```

A payment of £6,000 p.a. on a 25-year mortgage at 12% would allow you to borrow:

```
@PVAL(0.12,25,6000)= -£47,059
```

@NPER and **@IRATE** work back from the capital and the payment to find the number of periods and the interest rate. Both have an optional extended form:

```
@NPER(Rate,Pmt,Pv)
@NPER(Rate,Pmt,Pv,Fv,Type)

@IRATE(Nper,Pmt,Pv)
@IRATE(Nper,Pmt,Pv,Fv,Type)
```

Examples of all four of these functions can be seen in Figure 28.1. The formulae used here are:

```
B6:  @PAYMT(B4,B5,B3)
C3:  @PVAL(C4,C5,C6)
D5:  @NPER(D4,D6,D3)
E4:  @IRATE(E5,E6,E3)
```

■SECTION 28
Loans and investments

	A	B	C	D	E
1					
2		@PAYMT	@PVAL	@NPER	@IRATE
3	Capital	−50000	−47059	−50000	−50000
4	Interest Rate	12.0%	12.0%	12.0%	11.1%
5	No. Periods	25.0	25.0	28.4	25.0
6	Payment (annual)	6375.00	6000.00	6250.00	6000.00

Figure 28.1

Mortgages and tax relief

In practice, the real cost of mortgages and business loans is affected by the tax relief on interest. It is not difficult to extract the interest payment from the repayment of the principal – there are two functions **@IPAYMT** and **@PPAYMT** which do precisely that – but limitations on tax relief do complicate the issue. However, this is Quattro we're dealing with, and it can cope with anything.

The worksheet shown in Figure 28.2 calculates the mortgage repayments, net of tax relief, for domestic borrowers. As the relief is on interest on capital only, and limited to a ceiling of £30,000, no single formula will do the job. Columns C to F hold a table of the outstanding capital debt and the interest and capital components of the repayments over the 15-year span of the mortgage. By drawing on this, we can find the interest, and thence the tax relief, for any given year.

Two new functions are used in this table, **@IPAYMT** (the interest) and **@PPAYMT** (the capital repayment). Like the ordinary **@PAYMT** function they work from the present value, number of periods and interest rate, but they also need to know the number of the particular period for which the split is wanted. Their basic shapes are:

SECTION 28
Loans and investments

	A	B	C	D	E	F
1						
2						
3	Capital	50000	Year	Debt	@IPAYMT	@PPAYMT
4	Interest Rate	11.5%	1	50000	5750	1396
5	Years	15	2	48604	5589	1557
6	Annual Repayment	7146.22	3	47047	5410	1736
7			4	45311	5211	1935
8	Year No.	8	5	43376	4988	2158
9	Tax Threshold	30000	6	41218	4740	2406
10	Tax Free	30000	7	38812	4463	2683
11	Interest	3450	8	36129	4155	2991
12	Tax Rate	25%	9	33137	3811	3335
13	Tax Relief	862.50	10	29802	3427	3719
14			11	26083	3000	4147
15	Net Cost	6283.72	12	21936	2523	4624
16	Monthly	523.64	13	17313	1991	5155
17			14	12157	1398	5748
18			15	6409	737	6409

Figure 28.2

```
@IPAYMT(Rate,Period,Nper,Pv)
@PPAYMT(Rate,Period,Nper,Pv)
```

In the worksheet, the rate, number of periods and present value are all given as absolute references, linking to the cells at the top of the B column; the period numbers are taken from the 1...15 Year values in column C.

```
E4:  @IPAYMT($B$4,C4,$B$5,-$B$3)
F4:  @PPAYMT($B$4,C4,$B$5,-$B$3)
```

Column D values are generated by taking the outstanding capital debt and deducting from it the PPAYMT figure from the previous year:

```
D4: +B3                    {To start the series}
D5: +D4-F4                 {Last year debt - PPAYMT}
```

Most of the formulae used in Column B are straightforward. The Annual Repayment uses the standard @PAYMT function:

```
B6:  @PAYMT(B4,B5,-B3)
```

Finding the Tax Free component would be easy if it weren't for the £30,000 threshold – we could simply look up the remaining capital with the Year number as a reference:

```
@VLOOKUP(B8,C4..D19,1)       {B8 = Year No}
```

As it is, we must first check if the debt is above the threshold and use that if it is, the remaining debt if not:

```
B10: @IF(@VLOOKUP(B8,C4..D19,1)>B9,B9,@VLOOKUP(B8,C4..D19,1))
```

For the Interest value we could use the IPAYMT figure from column E – but only if it is below the threshold. Rather than write another @IF statement, we'll calculate the year's interest afresh. It is only a matter of multiplying the tax allowable sum by the interest rate:

```
B11: +B10*B4
```

For the Tax Relief, we multiply the interest by the appropriate tax rate – here set at 25%:

```
B13: +B11*B12
```

The Net Cost is arrived at by subtracting the tax relief from the annual repayment:

```
B15:  +B6-B13
```

Apply this to your own mortgage and tax position, and I guarantee it will come to a different answer. Fluctuating interest rates and the Building Society's special ways of calculating repayments are the causes. (And endowment mortgages are another problem.) However, it should be close enough for most purposes.

How much does it cost to borrow money with a credit card? When interest rates are quoted on a monthly basis, they can be deceptive – as many borrowers have found. Interest is calculated daily on the amount owing, and compounded monthly, so that the current 2.2% per month is actually equivalent to nearly 30% p.a. – over twice the nominal bank rate.

Figure 29.1 shows a worksheet that will work out the cost of an Access-style loan, and its APR (Annualised Percentage Rate). Only

```
             A              B        C

1    Credit Cards & Loan Sharks
2
3    Monthly Rate          2.2%
4    Amount                 100
5    From              30/04/91
6    To                29/07/91
7    Days                    90
8    Cost                  6.75
9
10   APR                  29.84%
11
12   Period           Capital   Interest
13                1      100        2.2
14                2    102.2     2.2484
15                3  104.4484  2.297865
16                4  106.7463  2.348418
17                5  109.0947  2.400083
18                6  111.4948  2.452885
19                7  113.9477  2.506848
20                8  116.4545  2.561999
21                9  119.0165  2.618363
22               10  121.6349  2.675967
23               11  124.3108  2.734838
24               12  127.0457  2.795005
25
26                     Total    29.8407
```

Figure 29.1

147

four items of data are needed – the interest rate, amount borrowed and the start and end dates. These latter must be properly entered as Date values so that the duration of the loan can be found by subtracting the one from the other.

Quattro's functions are of no help to us in these calculations, alas, and we shall have to revert to using the compound interest equation. This normally takes the form:

Future Value = Present Value * (1 + Rate) ^ Number of Periods

The way that it works can be seen in this simple example. Take a capital sum of £100 and an interest rate of 10%, over three years. The growth of the capital can be seen in the sequence:

	Capital	Interest @ 10%	End-of-year Capital
Year 1	£100.00	£10.00	£110.00
Year 2	£110.00	£11.00	£121.00
Year 3	£121.00	£12.10	£133.10

Put the same figures into the formula and you get:

$$£100 * (1 + 0.1) ^\wedge 3 = £100 * 1.1^\wedge 3 = £100 * 1.331$$
$$= £133.10$$

Subtract the initial capital from this and you have the total interest over the period. Substitute 0.022 (2.2%) for the interest rate and 12 months in place of 3 years, and you have the formula for calculating the APR:

```
B10:  (1+B3)^12-1
```

The 1 is subtracted at the end so that only the interest is left. That the APR of 29.84 is correct is proved by the month-by-month table

■ SECTION 29
Monthly interest and APR

in the lower part of Figure 29.1. That is generated by multiplying the each month's amount by the interest rate, and adding the interest in to the following month.

The Cost formula follows the same lines, but with an adjustment to convert the Days duration to Months. The expression Days/30 is sufficiently accurate here. That gives us:

$$Amount * (1 + Rate) \wedge (Days/30) - Amount$$

or:

```
B8:  +B4*(1+B3)^(B7/30)-B4
```

Structured loans

With these, the interest is charged on the initial amount throughout the period of the loan – even though the actual sum owed decreases steadily as payments are made. The quoted interest rate is normally several percent below the normal bank rate, but the APR is almost twice the quoted rate. The reason for this is fairly clear, and relates to that decreasing debt.

Suppose that you borrowed £50 for five months (interest free!) and paid it back at £10 per month. The debt would be:

Month 1	£50
Month 2	£40
Month 3	£30
Month 4	£20
Month 5	£10

Look at this another way. You could have borrowed £10 for 1 month, £10 for 2 months, £10 for 3 months, £10 for 4 months and another £10 for 5 months. It is the same as borrowing £10

■ SECTION 29
Monthly interest and APR

for 1+2+3+4+5 (=15) months, or £150 for 1 month, or £30 (the central figure) for the original 5-month term. By comparing the interest paid with that central figure, you get a far more realistic view of the rate.

A worksheet to calculate the APR is shown in Figure 29.2. Down to the Monthly Repayment (B9), the formulae are all simple arithmetic.

The Equivalent Loan (B10) is found by adding the initial loan and the monthly repayment (which is roughly equivalent to the amount owing at the start of the last month), then dividing by 2. Here it gives us (£1000 + £50) / 2 = £525. By comparing this to the annual interest, we get the first value for the APR:

```
B11: +B5/B10 {APR 1}
```

	A	B	C
1	Structured Loans		
2			
3	Loan	1000	
4	Rate	10.0%	
5	Annual Interest	100	+B3*B4
6	Term (Years)	2	
7	Total Interest	200	+B5*B6
8	Total Repayment	1200	+B3+B7
9	Monthly Repayment	50.00	+B8/(B6*12)
10	Equivalent Loan	525.00	(B3+B9)/2
11	APR 1	19.05%	+B5/B10
12			
13	@IRATE (Monthly)	1.51%	@IRATE(B6*12,B9,-B3)
14	APR 2	19.75%	(1+B13)^12-1

Figure 29.2

Monthly interest and APR

We can also tackle the problem using Quattro's @IRATE function. This will give us the monthly interest rate, working from the term in months, the repayments and the original loan:

```
B13:  @IRATE(B6*12,B9,-B3)
```

Here the function comes up with a rate of 1.51% per month. Compounding this to an annual rate, as we did earlier with the credit card loans, we get an APR of 19.75%.

```
B14:  (1+B13)^12-1 {APR 2}
```

The different approaches produce marginal different results, but in both cases, the APR comes out at nearly twice the nominal interest rate.

■ SECTION 30
Sales forecasts

With new products or in fast-changing markets, sales forecasts are largely guesswork. Good market research and the use of probability analysis can improve their reliability – then you've got educated guesswork. With an established product, numeric analysis is possible and can give a reasonable guide for the future.

Figure 30.1 shows a soft drinks firm's quarterly sales, in thousands of cans, over the last two years. A glance down the list will show that sales have varied substantially over the period but, on the whole, there is a rising trend. Closer examination will reveal a pattern, and this can be made much clearer by entering the numbers into a worksheet and graphing them. The resulting line graph is shown in Figure 30.2. (You may like to follow the layout of the worksheet in Figure 30.3, with the sales written into B4..B11. The later examples will use this sheet.)

Year	Quarter	Sales
1	1	685
	2	735
	3	764
	4	697
2	1	720
	2	772
	3	823
	4	768

Figure 30.1

The graph reveals a rising trend, with a clear seasonal variation – the sales peaking in the third quarter of each year. The questions now are how to quantify the underlying trend and how to produce seasonally-adjusted forecasts.

152

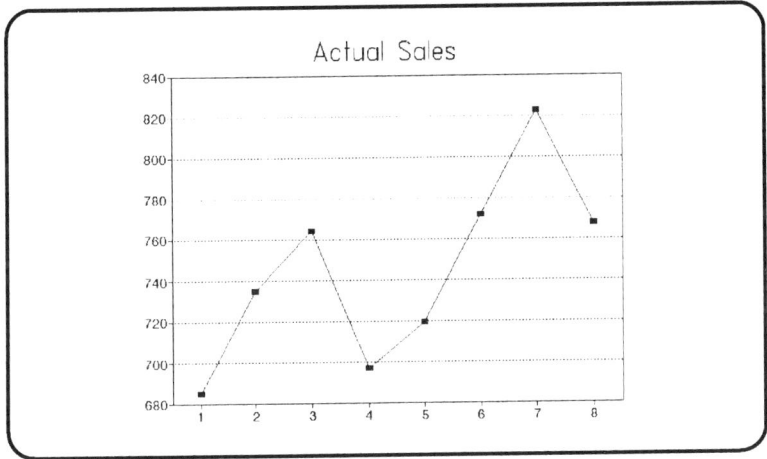

Figure 30.2

	A	B	C	D	E
1	Sales Forecasts				
2					
3	Quarter	Sales	Average	Variation	
4	1	685	685		Actual
5	2	735	710	50	
6	3	764	728	29	
7	4	697	720	-67	
8	5	720	729	23	
9	6	772	738	52	
10	7	823	753	51	
11	8	768	771	-55	
12	9	791	788	23	Forecast
13	10	842	806	51	
14	11	882	821	40	
15	12	821	834	-61	

Figure 30.3

■ SECTION 30
Sales forecasts

Moving averages

The function @AVG calculates the arithmetic average of the values in a block, i.e. the total divided by the number of values. Applied to the first year sales in our example, the function would read:

```
@AVG(B4..B7)
```

The result would be (685+735+764+697) / 4 = 2881 / 4 = 720. In the same way, we could get the average quarterly sales for the second year by @AVG(B8..B11). This gives us 771, and these two figures could be used as a basis for forecasting. The difference between them is 51; assuming that the growth continues at the same pace, we could add 51 to the second year's results to give us a projection for the current year. Let's return to this in a moment and focus on the trend.

To bring the trend line out, we need to smooth out the seasonal variation, and this can be done with Moving Averages – i.e. finding the average sales for the previous four quarters, each quarter. (Where there aren't four quarters – at the start of the list – we will have to make do by averaging as many results as are available.)

```
C6:  @AVG(B4..B6)  {last 3 quarters}
C7:  @AVG(B4..B7)  {last 4 quarters}
C8:  @AVG(B5..B8)  {last 4 quarters}
```

Graph these figures, and the underlying trend is quite clear. At the simplest, it could be projected by taking a pencil to the printed graph! (See Figure 30.4.)

Moving averages are probably more useful with weekly or monthly figures, and where there is more random variation, than with these limited and distinctly seasonal sales figures.

■ SECTION 30
Sales forecasts

Seasonal-adjusted forecasts

To make these, we must start by finding the quarterly variation in sales. Simple subtraction does the job:

```
D5:  +B5-B4
```

This formula is copied down to D11 to give the Actual Variation in column D. It is reasonable to assume that the seasonal fluctuations will follow much the same pattern in future. First, we will average the equivalent quarters in the two years:

```
D13:  (D5+D9)/2
```

Then add this to last known Sales figure to get the projection:

```
B13:  +B12+D13
```

Carried on down, this should give us a reliable forecast for each quarter of the coming year. Extend the Graph Series definition down to include the new data, and the resulting graph shows a consistent pattern (see Figure 30.4).

Forecasting should be an on-going process. Each quarter, the actual results should be entered, to replace the forecasts, and the projection taken on to the next quarter. The additional past data can be incorporated into the calculations to improve the reliability of the forecasts. Instead of averaging the last two equivalent quarters, you could work with the last three – or four, in time.

Average Spring Sales = (Spring1 + Spring2 + Spring3) / 3

It may also be useful to bring some weightings into the forecasts, to make last year's figures count for more than those from previous

Sales forecasts

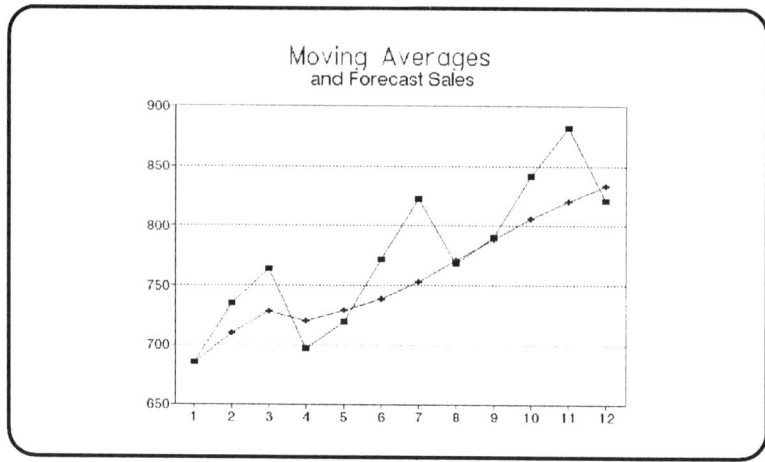

Figure 30.4

years. After all, the coming year will probably be more like last year than three years ago. The formula would then take the shape:

*Av. Spring Sales = (Spring1 + Spring2 * 2 + Spring3 * 3) / 6*

For example, suppose that the winter to spring variation had been:

Spring	Variation
Year 1	+10
Year 2	+30
Year 3	+50

A simple average would give us (10 + 30 + 50) / 3 = 30 for the increase this spring. A weighted average would produce:

    (10 + 30*2 + 50*3) / 6
= (10 + 60 + 150) /6
= 220 / 6
= 36.67

■ SECTION 31
Cashflow forecasts

The spreadsheet is an ideal tool for forecasting cashflows, as it makes it so easy to test 'What If?' situations. What if sales can be increased by 5% over the year? What if our new clients are slow payers? What if a payment is put off until another month? What if we invest in new machinery? When will it start to pay for itself and how do we cover the costs? What if we undertake this new project? How much of an overdraft will we need, and for how long?

You can ask these questions and work out the answers without a spreadsheet – but it takes so long! With a spreadsheet, you can run through a whole range of possibilities in the time that it would take you to process just one with a pocket calculator. (Mind you, there is some evidence to suggest that some managers get so wrapped up in their What If? permutations that they lose sight of their real work! But that is not the spreadsheet's fault.)

A cashflow worksheet need not be complex – it all depends upon the nature of the company's trading patterns. The example that is developed here is for a small manufacturing company, where almost all costs are directly related to sales (Figure 31.1). The relationships are written into the block B5..B11, at the top of the sheet. They show that Credit Sales make up 80% of all sales; that 70% of debts are paid within 30 days, another 25% within 60 days. (The remaining 5% being written off as bad debts.) They also show Purchases, Labour and Commission as percentages of the sales income. These cells are all named, for ease of reference within formulae (see block D4..E11).

The Sales figures have been estimated by the marketing people. There's a new product coming on-stream this Spring, and the initial promotion should result in a sales peak during May. Now these are only sales orders, not sales income. The cash from each month's sales will flow in over three months – cash sales immediately and credit sales one or two months later.

Cashflow forecasts

	A	B	C	D	E	F	G	H
1	Cash Flow Forecasts							
2	(Sales Related)							
3								
4		Percentages		Name Table				
5	Credit Sales	80%		BALANCE	B13			
6	30 day payments	70%		COMM	B11			
7	60 day payments	25%		CREDIT	B5			
8				GOODS	B9			
9	Purchases	35%		QUICK	B6			
10	Labour	30%		SLOW	B7			
11	Commission	5%		WORK	B10			
12								
13	Start Balance	-15000						
14								
15	Month	Jan	Feb	March	April	May	June	HALFYEAR
16	Sales	30000	30000	40000	60000	80000	60000	300000
17	Credit Sales	24000	24000	32000	48000	64000	48000	240000
18								
19	Credit Income	24000	22800	22800	28400	41600	56800	196400
20	Cash Income	6000	6000	8000	12000	16000	12000	60000
21	TOTAL INCOME	30000	28800	30800	40400	57600	68800	256400
22								
23	Outgoings							
24	Purchases	10500	14000	21000	28000	21000	21000	115500
25	Labour	9000	12000	18000	24000	18000	18000	99000
26	Commission	1500	1500	2000	3000	4000	3000	15000
27	Fixed Overheads	2000	2000	2000	2000	2000	2000	12000
28	Special Expenses	10000		8000				18000
29	TOTAL OUTGOING	33000	29500	51000	57000	45000	44000	259500
30								
31	NET FLOW	-3000	-700	-20200	-16600	12600	24800	
32	BALANCE	-18000	-18700	-38900	-55500	-42900	-18100	
33								
34	Debtors	30000					Net Debtors	61600

Figure 31.1

■ SECTION 31
Cashflow forecasts

The value of Credit sales is found by taking the credit percentage of the month's sales:

```
B17: +B16*$CREDIT
```

Each month's Credit Income will have two components: 70% of last month's sales, from the quick payers, and 25% of the previous month's (with estimates in the first two months to cover the debts from the previous year).

```
C19: +B17*$QUICK+6000 {6000 estimated old debts}
D19: +C17*$QUICK+B17*$SLOW
```

Cash Income is a simple matter of subtraction:

```
B20: +B16-B17 {Total sales - Credit sales}
```

And TOTAL INCOME is simple addition:

```
B21: +B19+B20
```

Purchases and Labour are based on percentages of the next month's sales – they have to be paid during the production of the articles:

```
B24: +C16*$GOODS
B25: +C16*$WORK
```

Commission, on the other hand, is due in the month of sales:

```
B26: [W8] +B16*$COMM
```

Fixed Overheads can be estimated from past experience, and the Special Expenses relate to planned purchases – £10,000 on

■ SECTION 31
Cashflow forecasts

equipment for the new product line in January, and a replacement van at £8,000 in March.

The TOTAL OUTGOINGS and NET FLOW formulae are as you would expect, and the running BALANCE uses similar formulae to those in the earlier Budgeting worksheet:

```
B29:  @SUM(B24..B28)
B31:  +B21-B29
B32:  +BALANCE+B31 {Start Balance + NET FLOW}
C32:  +B32+C31 {Last month's balance + NET FLOW}
```

All formulae are copied across the columns, for as many months as are required, and all are summed at the end.

There is one last formula, Net Debtors in H34. This gives the amount outstanding at the end of the period, by adding the slow payers from May's sales to both the quick and slow payers from June.

```
H34:  +G17*(QUICK+SLOW) +F17*SLOW
```

The bottom line of the cashflow in Figure 31.1 is that though the overdraft goes from bad to worse and back to bad, the underlying position does improve. By the end of the six months, the firm is showing a net inflow each month, and the outstanding debts are more than enough to cover the remaining overdraft. However, we live in times when banks tend to take an unsympathetic view of overdrafts, and our firm would have a better chance of living to see the summer if it kept its overdraft to less than £40,000. So what are the alternatives?

What If?

A worksheet is like a Lego set. Once you have built your model, you can start to play with it. Any cashflow projection must be hypothetical to some extent. Some costs and timings will be fixed, but others will offer some room for manoeuvre. It takes very little effort to key new values into the structure of relationships and formulae that you have created in a worksheet.

In the example developed in the last section, purchases of materials must remain at 35% of sales, given the established prices of both, nor can labour vary from its 30% costing, unless someone can come up with an effective productivity scheme. The £10,000 investment in new equipment in January is vital to the scheme, and fixed overheads are fixed. So what 'What Ifs?' can we do?

What if the purchase of a new van was put back a couple of months? We could delay it until May, but given the state of the current one, any later would be risking it. So, blank out D28 and write £8,000 into F28 – or use Edit I Move. By postponing the purchase until May, when the Net Flow at last becomes positive,

	A	B	C	D	E	F	G	H
1	Cash Flow Forecasts							
...								
14								
15	Month	Jan	Feb	March	April	May	June	HALFYEAR
...								
28	Special Expenses	10000				8000		18000
29	TOTAL OUTGOING	33000	29500	43000	57000	53000	44000	259500
30								
31	NET FLOW		-3000	-700	-12200	-16600	4600	24800
32	BALANCE		-18000	-18700	-30900	-47500	-42900	-18100
33								
34	Debtors		30000				Net Debtors	61600

Figure 32.1

we have reduced the worst excess of the overdraft – but still not enough. (See Figure 32.1.)

What if we could flatten out that hump of sales in May? The leap to £80,000 is all very well, but the production costs incurred for that are in April, while the bulk of the payments won't come in until June. What if we delay £10,000 of those sales until June? That will reduce the April overdraft by £6,000 in related costs. Unfortunately, it doesn't do much more than push the worst problem into May.

What if we pay the salesmen when the money comes in, not than when sales are made? Now this is a change of structure, rather than of values. The formulae that had calculated commission on row 16, will now have to do it on row 21:

```
B26: +B21 * $COMM
```

That helps a little, particularly in April and May:

	Jan	Feb	March	April	May	June
On sales	1500	1500	2000	3000	4000	3000
On payments	1575	1463	1569	2081	2825	3275

What if we could speed up the cash inflow by increasing the proportion of Cash sales or 30-day payments – or both? At this point, it is worth introducing Quattro's special **What-If** tool.

Tools I What-If

In essence, this allows you to substitute a range of alternative values into one or two key variables, and observe their effects on selected formulae. The alternative values and the results of the formulae are all held in a table.

As an example, we'll try varying the proportion of 30-day and 60-day payments and of Credit sales, and pick up the maximum overdraft and total Net Flow for the half-year. These two new formulae will act as a summary of the bottom line. 30- and 60-day payments can be varied by changing a single value, if we make one dependent upon the other. So, instead of the simple 0.25 in B7, we'll write a formula to subtract the 30-day figure from the total 95% of collectible credit sales:

```
B7:    0.95 - QUICK
```

One-variable analysis

1 Find a convenient corner of the sheet in which to construct the table. In the example, it has been located below the active area, starting at A37. The headings are unnecessary, but do help to make the results more meaningful (see Figure 32.2).

2 Write a set of alternative values for the key variable in the leftmost column. Here we want a range of percentages from 25% to 75%. The **Edit I Fill** command will do this quickly. The block is A38..A48, start value 0.25, step value 0.05. The figures are formatted as percentages for easy reading.

3 Write the results formulae into the top row of the table area. There must be at least one – otherwise there will be nothing to see! The formulae may be copies of ones elsewhere on the sheet, or written specifically for the What-If operation. In this case, the B column formulae will calculate the maximum overdraft – using the @MIN() function as we are after the lowest value; those in the C column will give the total Net Flow.

```
B38:  @MIN(B32..G32)
C38:  @SUM(B31..G31)
```

4 Pull down the **Tools** menu and select **What-If 1 Variable**.

5 Define the data table to include the list of alternative values and those columns headed by a results formula. Here the block is `A38..C48`.

6 When asked for the `Input Cell for column`, point to the cell that will take the alternative values from the column. In the example this will be B6 – the 30-day payment cell.

7 Wait for a moment for the table to be built. The blank cells in the table will be filled with the results produced by the formulae at the top of the columns, when the Input Cell had the value on that row. For example, on row 40 of Figure

	A	B	C
....			
37	30 Days	Max O/D	Net Flow
38	25%	-62500	-30400
39	30%	-60100	-27600
40	35%	-57700	-24800
41	40%	-55300	-22000
42	45%	-52900	-19200
43	50%	-50500	-16400
44	55%	-48100	-13600
45	60%	-45700	-10800
46	65%	-43300	-8000
47	70%	-40900	-5200
48	75%	-38500	-2400

Figure 32.2

32.2, the maximum overdraft would be £57,700 and the net flow -£24,800 when 35% of debts were paid within 30 days.

The table shows very clearly that the overdraft shrinks, and net flow improves, as the proportion of 30-day payments is increased. If the firm can push it to 75%, they should be able to keep within their £40,000 limit.

Two-variable analysis

Though substantially the same as the one-variable version, there are some critical differences in the way that this operates. The most noticeable of these is that the table will only show the results from one formula.

1 Find a convenient spot below or to the right of the active sheet.

2 Write a list of alternative values for the first variable down the left-hand column, leaving the top cell blank. Here the list from the previous example is being pressed back into service.

3 Write the values for the second variable across the top row. In this example, we are going to vary the proportion of Credit sales, over the range of 60% to 90% (B37..G37 in Figure 32.3).

4 Write the results formula into the top left cell. In this case, it is @MIN(B32..G32).

5 Define the data table to include the column and row of alternative values.

What If?

	A	B	C	D	E	F	G	H
. . . .								
37	−36250	60%	65%	70%	75%	80%	85%	90%
38	25%	−38500	−44500	−50500	−56500	−62500	−68500	−74500
39	30%	−36700	−42550	−48400	−54250	−60100	−65950	−71800
40	35%	−34900	−40600	−46300	−52000	−57700	−63400	−69100
41	40%	−33100	−38650	−44200	−49750	−55300	−60850	−66400
42	45%	−31300	−36700	−42100	−47500	−52900	−58300	−63700
43	50%	−29500	−34750	−40000	−45250	−50500	−55750	−61000
44	55%	−27700	−32800	−37900	−43000	−48100	−53200	−58300
45	60%	−25900	−30850	−35800	−40750	−45700	−50650	−55600
46	65%	−24200	−28900	−33700	−38500	−43300	−48100	−52900
47	70%	−23000	−26950	−31600	−36250	−40900	−45550	−50200
48	75%	−21800	−25450	−29500	−34000	−38500	−43000	−47500

Figure 32.3

6 Define the Input Cell for column as before, giving the reference of the first variable – here the 30-day payment cell, B6.

7 Point to the second variable's cell – here Credit Sales in B5 – for the Input Cell for top row.

8 Wait for a moment. Depending upon the size of the table and the complexity of the worksheet, this can take time. The table displays the values of the top left formula produced by each combination of the alternative Input Cell values.

In the example in Figure 32.3, we can see in B43 that the maximum overdraft will be £29,500 when 60% of sales are on credit and 50% of these are paid within 30 days. We can also see that there are a number of options that will allow us to keep the overdraft below £40,000. We could draw a diagonal line from B38 to F48, and take any combination below that line. Speed of payment is almost irrelevant if we can manage to hold credit sales to 60% or less, but as this proportion rises, so we must ensure that a higher proportion of payments come in quicker.

Figure 32.4 shows the final version of the cashflow, incorporating the various What Ifs? Target proportions for credit sales and 30 day payments have been set at 75% and 70% respectively, the best that the sales staff think can be achieved. With the other alterations, this leaves the firm with an acceptable level of overdraft.

	A	B	C	D	E	F	G	H
1	Cash Flow Forecasts							
2	(Sales Related)							
3								
4		Percentages		Name Table		Changes		
5	Credit Sales	75%		BALANCE	B13	Credit Sales to 75%		
6	30 day payments	70%		COMM	B11	Commission in arrears		
7	60 day payments	25%		CREDIT	B5	May June averaged		
8				GOODS	B9	New van moved to May		
9	Purchases	35%		QUICK	B6			
10	Labour	30%		SLOW	B7			
11	Commission	5%		WORK	B10			
12								
13	Start Balance	−15000						
14								
15	Month	Jan	Feb	March	April	May	June	Total
16	Sales	30000	30000	40000	60000	70000	70000	300000
17	Credit Sales	22500	22500	30000	45000	52500	52500	225000
18								
19	Credit Income	24000	21750	21375	26625	39000	48000	180750
20	Cash Income	7500	7500	10000	15000	17500	17500	75000
21	TOTAL INCOME	31500	29250	31375	41625	56500	65500	255750
22								
23	Outgoings							
24	Purchases	10500	14000	21000	24500	24500	21000	115500
25	Labour	9000	12000	18000	21000	21000	18000	99000
26	Commission	1575	1463	1569	2081	2825	3275	12788
27	Fixed Overheads	2000	2000	2000	2000	2000	2000	12000
28	Special Expenses	10000				8000		18000
29	TOTAL OUTGOING	33075	29463	42569	49581	58325	44275	257288
30								
31	NET FLOW	−1575	−213	−11194	−7956	−1825	21225	
32	BALANCE	−16575	−16788	−27981	−35938	−37763	−16538	
33								
34	Debtors	30000				Net Debtors		63000

Figure 32.4

■ SECTION 33
Solving problems

In this section we will explore another tool for finding optimum values. **Solve For** takes an end-on approach – you specify what it is that you are looking for, and Quattro finds the value that will produce the result.

The classic example of a problem that benefits from this approach is the Director's Bonus. This may well be a set percentage of the final profit – which is calculated after deduction of the bonus! It is a circular problem. You could solve it by repeated recalculation.

The double-sided relationship between bonus and profit can be set up easily enough – it just needs a pair of formulae like those in cells C4 and C5 of Figure 33.1. When these are first written they will show £0 for the bonus and £1,050,000 for the profit, assuming that the bonus formula is written first. Recalculate it and the bonus will become £52,500, with the profit reduced to £997,500. Keep on pressing [F9] to recalculate – or set the **Options I Recalculate I Iteration** to 10 or so – and eventually you will get the right answers of £50,000 for the bonus and £1,000,000 for the profit. (The number of recalculations depends upon the level of accuracy desired. In this case, four iterations will get you to the nearest pound, seven to the nearest penny.)

```
        A        B        C        D
1    The Directors Bonus
2
3    Profit             1050000
4    Directors Bonus    0.05*C5
5    Net Profit         +C3-C4
```

Figure 33.1

```
          A        B        C        D
  1    The Directors Bonus
  2
  3    Profit             1050000
  4    Directors Bonus      50000 << Variable Cell
  5    Net Profit         1000000
  6
  7    5% of Profit         50000
  8    Difference         -1.8E-06 << Formula Cell
  9
 10                               Target Value 0
 11
```

Figure 33.2

To tackle this problem with the **Solve For** tool, we need a slightly different set of formulae. There must be a cell which is either blank or contains only a simple value, into which Quattro can enter values while working towards a solution. Quattro also needs a target, which must be a straight numerical value. You cannot write in 0.05*PROFIT, or any other formula as the target. Lastly, there must be a formula to which this target relates: i.e. the problem to be solved. For the Director's Bonus, the sheet could be rebuilt on the lines shown in Figure 33.2.

The problem is to find a Bonus value which is equal to 5% of the profit after the bonus has been deducted. This can be expressed simplest by writing the Bonus and the 5% calculation into two cells and comparing the difference between them. When the difference is 0, then the problem is solved. That translates to the following set-up for the cells:

```
    C4:  blank      Solve For will fill this in for us
    C5:  +C3-C4     As in Figure 32.1
    C7:  0.05*C5    As in C4 in Figure 32.1
    C8:  +C4-C7     The target formula to be solved
```

169

Using the Solve For Tool

1 Pull down the **Tools** Menu and select **Solve For**.

2 For the **Formula Cell** give the reference of the cell containing the target formula – here it is C8, the Difference.

3 For the **Target** give the value that you want to see in the Formula Cell. In this case it will be 0.

4 For the **Variable Cell** give the cell where you want Quattro to try out values as it hunts for a solution – C4 in this case.

5 Select **Go** to run the operation, then **Quit** to return to the sheet.

In this simple example, Solve For comes up with a result that is more than accurate enough for all practical purposes. (The difference of -1.8E-06 represents roughly ⅟₅₀₀ of a penny.) Sometimes, however, Solve For will not produce a satisfactory answer the first time that it is used. This may be because the problem is to complex to be solved accurately within the normal limitations of operation. These can be altered.

The **Parameters** option of the Solve For menu allows you to set **Max Iterations** – the number of recalculations – at anything from 1 to 99; and the **Accuracy** – how close you want to get to the Target. The defaults are five iterations, which are usually enough, and an accuracy of 0.005, which may well be overdoing it. In money terms, 0.005 is a halfpenny!

Solving problems

Solve For will also fail if the target is unrealistic. We could have used this tool with the Cashflow worksheet to work back from the overdraft to the credit sales. We had already established that different proportions of 30-day payments had a direct effect on the overdraft levels. So why not set a target overdraft and find a 30-day percentage that will deliver that.

The **Formula Cell** would be one containing @MIN(B32..G32), i.e. the largest overdraft; the **Variable Cell** would be the 30-day percentage. Running a variety of **Targets** through the routine produces these results:

Target	30-day percentage
-50000	39%
-40000	62%
-30000	84%
-25000	108% !!!!!
0	- No result -

The last run produced the Error Message 'Solve For is not converging on a solution' – the overdraft will not disappear, no matter how much you fiddle with the credit payments. The penultimate run was also unsatisfactory in that 108% is impossible – but this is a judgment for you to make. It is always worth remembering that a worksheet is quite capable of delivering nonsense to a very high level of accuracy.

PART SEVEN

Working with multiple worksheets

■ SECTION 34
Between the sheets

So far, we have taken worksheets one at a time, but Quattro Pro can cope with any number at a time, and on a flexible basis. They may simply sit side by side in memory, with no connection between them save for your interest; they may be linked so that data passes from sheet to sheet; or they may be joined into a *workspace* system. There is no real limit on how many sheets may be open at once; Quattro's excellent VROOM memory management seems to adopt a more-the-merrier principle. (It never fails to impress me, when I've loaded in a third or fourth large sheet, to find that I have more memory available than there was before!)

There are a number of advantages in splitting a job over several sheets rather than tackling it as a single massive one. Smaller sheets are quicker to load into memory and much easier to manage. You are less likely to get lost on them; you don't need to take the sellotape to the printouts; and there will be fewer names to remember (or forget). Where the sheets cover the work of different departments or individuals, they can be farmed out for updating and maintenance, and brought back together to produce the summary. Where the sheets relate to different months or years, those that are not needed for the job in hand can be left on disk, but all loaded in on those rarer occasions when a long-term view is required.

Linked sheets
Data can be passed from one sheet to another by making links with extended references. These have the sheet name written in square brackets, immediately before the cell reference. The cells may be identified by row and column references, though it is usually simpler to use names. [DEPT1]A15, [DEPT1]B15, [SALES]TOTAL and [STOCK]$MARKUP would all be valid references – assuming that there are sheets called 'DEPT1', 'SALES' and 'STOCK', and that those names exist.

■ SECTION 34
Between the sheets

The sheet from which data is being drawn by a link is called a *supporting* sheet. It would normally by present in memory when the reference is first written and later when its data is used – but this is not essential. The cell may initially display NA, to indicate that the data is Not Available, but given the right command (see *Updating Links*, below), Quattro will track down the reference in the file on disk, and pass the data back up through the link. The value is then retained in the master sheet for the rest of the work session.

The fact that supporting sheets do not have to be in memory for their values to be accessed is of great advantage to networked users. People can work on supporting sheets independently while the linked master sheet is active elsewhere.

Updating links
Whenever you open a file that contains links to other sheets – and those sheets are not currently in memory – you will be presented with the **Link options** menu. There are three options.

■ **Load Supporting** brings all linked sheets into memory.

■ **Update References** collects the relevant values from the disk files, but leaves those other sheets closed.

■ **None** opens no other sheets and results in linked cells displaying NA.

Once a master sheet is open, its links to other sheets can be modified through the **Tools I Update** command. This offers four options.

■ **Open** is equivalent to **Load Supporting**, except that you can choose which of the linked sheets are opened. This is managed via a menu window that displays the names of referenced sheets and invites you to Pick one or more worksheets. To pick just one sheet, highlight it and press [Return]. To pick several, highlight each in turn and press [Shift]-[F7]. A tick appears beside the name, and when you press [Return] the ticked sheets are opened.

■ **Refresh** is equivalent to **Update References**, but with the same Pick one or more... option.

■ **Change** allows you to switch all references from one sheet to another. This could be very useful if you have sheets with identical structure but different data, and you only want to draw one department's or year's results into the master sheet at a time.

■ **Delete** lets you remove all references to a currently linked sheet – they are replaced by ERR messages.

File commands for multiple sheets
Individual sheets within a multiple sheet environment respond to the normal **File I Save** and **Retrieve**, but others now come into play. The following commands relate principally to second and subsequent sheets.

■ **File I New** sets up a blank sheet, while leaving any existing sheets present in memory. The new sheet is the *current* one – the one containing the cursor.

■ **File I Open** is equivalent to **New** followed by **Retrieve**. Existing sheets are unaffected, but pushed into the background. If the new sheet contains links to other sheets still on disk, the **Link options** menu will pop up.

■SECTION 34
Between the sheets

■ **File I Close** shuts down the current sheet. If it has been edited since its last Save, you will be warned that changes will be lost and given the chance to back out. After the Close, the next worksheet in the pile becomes current. If you Close the last remaining sheet, the screen blanks, leaving only a restricted **File** menu. This only offers New, Open, File Manager and Exit options.

■ **File I Save All** saves all open sheets – collecting filenames for new sheets and offering the usual **Cancel**, **Replace** and **Backup** options for those already on disk.

■ **File I Close All** likewise works on all the sheets, offering a **Save and Close** option on any sheet that has been changed.

The workspace concept
Where a set of sheets – linked or not – are regularly used together, they can be conveniently joined into a workspace. This is essentially a file which lists the names of the worksheets in the set, and is identified by a WSP extension.

■ **File I Workspace Save** joins all the currently open sheets into a workspace. *It does not save the sheets.*

■ **File I Workspace Restore** opens all the sheets in the selected workspace. For some reason this always takes an inordinate amount of time, with much chopping and changing between the sheets as they load.

■SECTION 35
Windows and screen displays

Worksheets and windows

In Quattro jargon, it is not worksheets that you have on the screen, but windows. The distinction is subtle but real. A *window* is a view onto a sheet, and it is possible to have the same sheet open in more than one window. Quattro will alert you if you try to open a sheet that is already open, as there is a danger of confusion and data loss. If you make changes in two copies of the same sheet, only one set of changes will be saved.

So, even though worksheets and windows are virtually synonymous, for all practical purposes we'll stick to the term 'windows' when talking about displays and on-screen activities.

The Windows menu

A window initially occupies the whole screen, but this can be changed easily enough. The size and position of each window can be individually controlled, and multi-window displays can be called up by a single keystroke. The commands can be found on the Windows menu. They are all fairly straightforward, but it is worth opening up three or four windows and having a play with these commands, before you use them in earnest.

■ **Windows I Tile** (shortcut [Ctrl]-[T]) divides the screen into multiple windows, each with a title line and the row/column headings (Figure 35.1). The active sheet's window is indicated by a double outline and the presence of the cursor. The command always makes a window for each open sheet – whether you want to view it or not – and allocates space by simple division of the screen – even though you may have previously adjusted their size.

In theory, you can have up to 32 windows open, and on screen at once. In practice, on a CGA (80x25) screen, once you get beyond three of four windows, there's not much to see in any

■ SECTION 35
Windows and screen displays

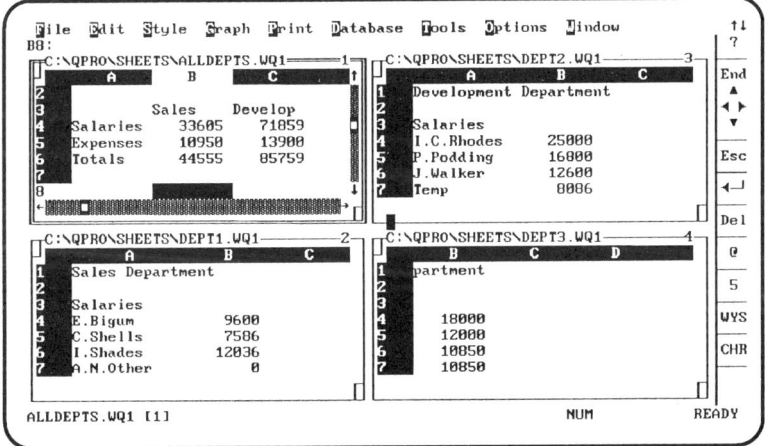

Figure 35.1

of them. The 43-line EGA and 50-line VGA screens can cope
with proportionately more, but the smaller the windows, the
more difficult it is to find your way around a sheet.

Tile is a one-way command. You cannot simply cancel it to
restore each window to its full size.

■ **Windows I Zoom** ([Alt]-[F6]) expands the current window to fill
the whole screen. This is a two-way command. Use it on a
full-size window and it shrinks back to its previous size.

■ **Windows I Stack** arranges all open windows, so that the top
lines of the underlying sheets are visible, and writes the sheet
name and window number into these lines. It is a useful
reminder of which sheets are open, and takes relatively little
space.

■SECTION 35
Windows and screen displays

■ **Windows|Move/Size** (shortcut [Ctrl]-[R]) gives you in-
dividual control of the position and size of the current window.
The system will initially be in **Move** mode – indicated by the
word 'MOVE' in the top left corner. Toggle between this and **Size**
by pressing [Scroll Lock].

Move will only work if the window is less than full-size, and
no window can be moved so that its border goes off-screen.

In **Size** mode, the top left corner of the window is fixed and
the cursor keys (or mouse) move the bottom and right edges.

■ **Windows|Pick** displays the names of open sheets and their
window numbers, and invites you to select one. In practice,
it is quicker and simpler to do this direct from the keyboard
or with the mouse (see below).

Window panes

The window analogy is taken further by the concept of *panes*. A
window can be split either vertically or horizontally into two panes,
each of which can be moved independently over the sheet. This is
very useful when you are doing 'What Ifs' on a large worksheet,
as you can bring the data entry and results area into view at the
same time. Where there are several open windows, each can be
split into panes separately.

The commands that control the panes make up the bulk of the
Windows|Options sub-set.

■ **Windows|Options Horizontal** splits the window at the row
containing the cursor. If it is already split, nothing happens.

■ **Windows|Options Vertical** splits the window at the column
containing the cursor.

■ SECTION 35
Windows and screen displays

■ **Windows I Options Sync** synchronises the panes in the direction of the split; i.e. with horizontal panes, the columns will be aligned and will move together once the cursor reaches the edge of the screen.

■ **Windows I Options Unsync** releases the panes so that each may be moved independently.

■ **Windows I Options Clear** restores the single window.

The keyboard and the mouse
Where a window has been split into panes, mouse users can switch between them simply by pointing and clicking. They can move to different windows in the same way, as long as at least part of the desired window is visible. Working from the keyboard is almost as simple.

■ **[F6]** jumps to the opposite pane of the current window.

■ **[Shift]-[F6]** jumps to the **Next Window** – 'next' being determined by the order of loading.

■ **[Shift]-[F5]** and **[Alt]-[0]** are both alternatives to the **Window I Pick** command, and work in exactly the same way.

You can also move directly to a given window by pressing [Alt] and the window number – assuming that you can remember what it is.

Titles and other Window options
The last few options are largely concerned with tweaking the screen display, but should not be ignored. Each of these affects only the current window, or the current pane in a split window.

■ SECTION 35
Windows and screen displays

■ **Windows | Options Locked Titles** fixes the top row(s) and/or leftmost column(s) so that they do not move when the worksheet is scrolled. This will keep headings in view as you move across the largest sheets. Before calling up the command, move the cursor to the cell below the rows, or to the right of the columns to be immobilised. There are three alternatives: **Horizontal**, **Vertical** and **Both**. Once a part of the screen has been locked, you can only get to its cells – perhaps to edit a label – by **Clearing** the titles or by using **GoTo** to jump to a specific cell.

■ **Windows | Options Row and Col Borders** allows you to remove the borders from the display. This can be handy with multi-window displays as it slightly increases the amount of space for data.

■ **Windows | Map View** gives an overview of the sheet, with the columns reduced to one character wide and the contents of the occupied cells represented by symbols denoting their contents:

l	Label
n	Number
+	Formula
-	Link to another sheet
g	Inserted graph
c	Circular reference

Map View is a debugging tool. It helps you to check that the structure of formulae is complete and to track down linking formulae and those containing circular references. It is best used in one pane of a split sheet. That makes it much easier to check the displayed values and the actual contents of cells.

■ SECTION 35
Windows and screen displays

■ **Windows | Grid Lines** is purely for the WYSIWYG mode, giving you control of the display of the grid lines between the cells. They are pretty, but rather a waste of space.

Right, enough of the theory and the commands, let's get some multiple worksheets into use.

■ SECTION 36
Linked budgets

In this section we'll develop a departmental budgeting system. Though highly simplified, its basic structure and method of construction can be applied to real business situations. In essence the system consists of a sheet for each department with a master sheet containing summary information.

Start with the worksheet for one of the departments, but designed with flexibility in mind. As the same type of data and calculations will be needed in each, it should be possible to adapt the first sheet to suit the other departments, and quicker to do this than to create each from scratch. Figure 36.1 shows the sheet for the Sales department, with the formulae written beside the cells. Note that both the @SUM ranges extend beyond the active cells, to make it simpler to insert extra rows if needed. The firm's pension and

	A	B	
1	Sales Department		
2			
3	Salaries		
4	E.Bigum	9000	
5	C.Shells	7586	
6	I.Shades	12036	
7	A.N.Other	0	
8			
9	Sub-Total	28622	@SUM(B4..B8)
10	N.I.	3148	+B9*0.11
11	Pension	1145	+B9*0.04
12	TOTAL	32915	+B9+B10+B11
13			
14	Expenses		
15	Rent	5000	
16	Heat & Light	1200	
17	Depreciation	2500	
18	Maintenance	750	
19	Sundries	1500	
20			
21	TOTAL	10950	@SUM(B15..B20)

Figure 36.1

184

■ SECTION 36
Linked budgets

National Insurance contributions are here calculated at 4% and 11% of gross pay. At this stage, the only entries on the worksheet should be those formulae and headings that are common to all departments. Specific data should be left until the basic sheet has been copied for other departments.

There are two ways to copy a worksheet. You can save the sheet, then open it again and save it under a new name – or save the sheet several times under different names. The other way is to use an extended Copy. Try this to set up the second and later worksheets:

1 Open a new window with **File I New**.

2 Use **Pick** or **Next Window** to return to the first sheet.

3 Call up **Edit I Copy** and define the block to be copied – in this case from A1 to the furthest occupied cell.

4 When asked for the destination, use **Pick** or **Next Window** to go to the new sheet. Its name will appear in the entry line.

5 Complete the destination definition by pointing to the top left cell. Press [Return] to complete.

Single cells and partial blocks can equally well be copied from sheet to sheet. The formulae remain intact, and cell references will be adjusted to suit a change of position, as normal.

Once the basic structure has been copied across the set, each sheet can be varied – by inserting or deleting rows – to suit the department's requirements. Specific headings, labels and the necessary data can then be added. (Compare Figures 36.1 and 36.2.)

In this example, only two figures will be passed from each supporting sheet to the summary. These are the TOTALs for Salaries and Expenses. For ease of handling, the cells should be named – SALARIES and EXPENSES will do nicely. The same names can be conveniently used in every sheet. There will be no confusion, as the sheet name will be included in the references.

When complete, the sheets should be saved with unambiguous and easily remembered names – SALES, DEVELOP, PRODUCT,

	A	B	
1	Development Department		
2			
3	Salaries		
4	I.C.Rhodes	25000	
5	P.Podding	17500	
6	J.Walker	12600	
7			
8	Sub-Total	63186	@SUM(B4..B7)
9	N.I.	6950	+B8*0.11
10	Pension	2527	+B8*0.04
11	TOTAL	72664	+B8+B9+B10
12			
13	Expenses		
14	Rent	3000	
15	Heat & Light	800	
16	Depreciation	4500	
17	Maintenance	2000	
18	Sundries	3600	
19			
20	TOTAL	13900	@SUM(B14..B19)

Figure 36.2

Linked budgets

STORES, etc. Leave them all open while the master sheet is written.

The master sheet

In this example, all we will do is pull the totals in from each sheet, and add them up to get totals for the firm. For practical work, you would probably want to include some form of analysis and comparisons with budget targets.

The basic layout is shown in Figure 36.3. To create this we would open up a fresh sheet with **File | New**, then type in the headings. Linking references will generally have to be written individually – copying will adjust the row/column references (inappropriately) and not change the sheet names. The use of named cells does at least mean that you do not have to keep switching to other sheets to look up references.

```
B4:  +[SALES]SALARIES
B5:  +[SALES]EXPENSES
C4:  +[DEVELOP]SALARIES
C5:  +[DEVELOP]EXPENSES
D4:  +[PRODUCT]SALARIES
D5:  +[PRODUCT]EXPENSES
```

	A	B	C	D	E
1	Costs 1990-91				
2					
3		Sales	Develop	Product	All Depts
4	Salaries	32915	72664	94306	199885
5	Expenses	10950	13900	16700	41550
6	Totals	43865	86564	111006	241435
7					

Figure 36.3

■ SECTION 36
Linked budgets

As the links are entered, the referenced values are drawn in, and these are updated automatically as changes are made to supporting sheets. To test this, use **Windows I Tile** to bring all the sheets into view, then note the results on the master sheet as new values are typed elsewhere.

When the master sheet has been completed and saved, the whole set can be saved as a workspace. Simply call up **File I Workspace Save**. At the end of the session, use **File I Close All** and take advantage of the Save option as it is offered on those sheets that have been edited.

■ SECTION 37
Customer accounts and invoices

In this second example of multi-sheet working, it is no longer possible to talk in terms of master and supporting sheets, for here the transfer of data is two-way.

The system produces invoices and updates the customers' accounts. At any one point, three worksheets will be active: the stock list, the invoice and the account sheet. This latter will be one selected from a set, for each customer has his own worksheet. That creates a small, though easily solved, problem.

In use, the invoice template worksheet would first be opened, followed by the stock sheet – the two could conveniently be joined in a workspace. The accounts clerk would then open the sheet for the current customer, and update the links so that the relevant formulae pointed to that sheet. The cross links between the two sheets will copy the customer's details into the invoice, and the summary data from the invoice will be copied back into the customer account sheet. In the version developed here, the user would need to be familiar with a few Quattro commands to handle the system, but in the next part of the book you will see how a set of short macros could make it even simpler to use.

As the sheets are interdependent, they are best written in parallel. We'll start with the invoice worksheet. This is based on the sheet developed in Section 27. You might like to load up your version and work through the process. The first job is to lop off the lookup table and make that into a new sheet. This can be done by using **File | New** to open a new sheet then copy the block into it. As an alternative, you could *Extract* the table – take part of the sheet and save it as a new file.

Using Tools | Extract

1 Pull down the **Tools** menu and select **Extract**.

■ SECTION 37
Customer accounts and invoices

2 You will be offered the choice of **Formulae** or **Values**. In this case, only values are wanted.

3 Define the block to be saved.

4 Give a suitable filename for the new sheet. We might call this CATFISH as it is a catalogue of fish. The sheet is saved to disk, but not opened at that time. It is needed here, so should be opened now. The new sheet is shown in Figure 37.1.

5 If the extracted block is no longer wanted on the original sheet, use **Edit I Erase** to remove it.

Tools I Extract will happily copy formulae into the new sheet, with the normal adjustments of references to suit the change in

```
           A            B            C
   1    Stock List

   2
   3    Code         Type          Price
   4             1 Large Cod       £2.45
   5             2 Small Cod       £2.37
   6             3 Haddock         £2.67
   7             4 Smoked Haddock  £4.30
   8             5 Coley           £1.15
   9             6 Mackerel        £2.79
  10             7 Shrimps         £3.90
  11             8 Lobster         £4.65
  12             9 Crab            £3.60
  13            10 Mussels         £2.75
  14
```

Figure 37.1

position. Names, however, are not transferred and must be created anew if required. It will need doing here and we may as well re-use the previous name – TABLE.

First alterations to the invoice worksheet

Having extracted the lookup table and erased it from the invoice, we will have to rewrite the lookup formulae to include the worksheet name. The new version of the Type and Unit Price lookups should read:

```
C11:  @IF(B11>0,@VLOOKUP(B11,[CATFISH]$TABLE,1),"")
D11:  @IF(B11>0,@VLOOKUP(B11,[CATFISH]$TABLE,2),"")
```

Note that an absolute reference ($TABLE) is used so that the formulae can be copied successfully.

Before starting on the customer sheet, we could usefully prepare the invoice sheet to make linking easier (Figure 37.2). Two items of data will be passed to the customer's account: the date and the total. Each of these should be named – DATE and TOTAL will do nicely. Finally, the altered sheet should be saved under a new name. I have called it INBASE, as it is the base sheet for all invoices.

The Customer Account sheets

As with the invoices, these can be produced from a single template worksheet that contains the core structure of headings, formulae and named cells. We want the sheet to record a summary of each invoice, payments made, the amounts owing and the age of the debts. It should also show totals of the sales and payments, and check the sum outstanding against a credit limit.

Figure 37.3 shows the sheet after three invoices and two payments have been recorded. It is designed to grow as it is used. For each

Customer accounts and invoices

```
       A    B         C            D           E          F        G
   1        INVOICE PREPARATION
   2

   3        TOWZER'S FISH SALE        To:    Fission Chips
   4        Dock Street                      Seaview St
   5        Grimsby                          Cleethorpes
   6        Tel: 0472 123456                 0472 654321

   7
   8        Date: 03/03/91          Inv. No. 921234
   9

  10        Code Type              Unit Price  Qty       Cost

  11           2 Small Cod            £2.37      15      £35.55
  12           5 Coley                £1.15      20      £23.00
  13           6 Mackerel             £2.79      12      £33.48
  14          10 Mussels              £2.75      10      £27.50
  15           3 Haddock              £2.67      30      £80.10
  16           7 Shrimps              £3.90       5      £19.50
  17                                                      £0.00
  18                                                      £0.00
  19                                                      £0.00
  20                                                      £0.00

  21                                          Sub total £219.13
  22                               Discount     10.00%   £21.91

  23                                          GOODS     £241.04

  24                               Weight          92
  25                               Carriage @    0.26    £23.46

  26                                          TO PAY    £264.50

  27

  28
```

Figure 37.2

Customer accounts and invoices

	A	B	C	D	E	F	G
1	Fission Chips						
2	Seaview St						
3	Cleethorpes						
4	0472 654321						
5							
6	Credit Limit	500					
7							
8	Inv. No.	Date	InvTotal	Pay Date	Amount	Due	Age of Debt
9	915432	13/02/91	413.65	28/01/91	413.65	0.00	
10	915435	13/03/91	181.15	04/03/91	181.15	0.00	
11	921234	02/05/91	264.50			264.50	54
12						0.00	
13			859.303		594.8	264.50	
14							

Figure 37.3

new invoice a row will be inserted within the record area – the next one would go between rows 11 and 12 – and linking formulae copied into the row. We'll get back to that shortly.

Columns B and D are formatted as **Dates**, column A as **Fixed 0** and the rest of the sheet as **Fixed 2**. The formulae are all either straightforward linked references or calculations, though they are used in a slightly less straightforward way.

The Invoice Number will be keyed in by the user. It could be linked, but that would create problems in later formulae.

The Date and InvTotal are drawn in by linked references. Note that these are encased in @IF statements so that the cells will remain blank if there is no invoice number present.

```
B12:  @IF(A12>0,[INBASE]$DATE,"")
C12:  @IF(A12>0,[INBASE]$TOTAL,"")
```

By capturing the data before the invoice sheet is saved under a new name, we can conveniently use INBASE. This does mean however, that if the links were left intact, they would update with each invoice – losing their old data! The solution lies in the way that the sheet is used.

Copies of these two formulae, and those in later columns, are written in the bottom row – here it is row 12. When a row is inserted for a new invoice, the formulae are all copied into it. The invoice number is typed into the first column, activating the links for the date and total. The contents of those cells are then copied back onto themselves – *as values* – overwriting the links with actual numbers. The command for this is **Edit I Values**, which takes a source block and destination in the same way as Copy. With the sheet as in Figure 37.3, the command line would be:

```
/Edit|Values, B11..C11, B11
```

When a payment is made, the user would enter the Pay Date and Amount in columns D and E of the relevant row. The Due value is then found by simple subtraction – e.g. `C12-E12`.

The **Age of Debt** is calculated using the @TODAY function and the date value in column B, and is thus automatically up to date. It's wrapped in an @IF statement to make it ignore fully paid invoices:

```
@IF(F12>0,TODAY = 2,"")
```

The bottom line totals for InvTotal, Amount and Due are all simple @SUM(...) formulae. Define the blocks so that they include the title line and the lowest (blank) line of formulae. This will give greatest flexibility later.

■ SECTION 37
Customer accounts and invoices

All that is left now, is to create the names that will make it easier to carry the customer details back from here to the INBASE worksheet. There are only four cells, up in the top left:

Cell	Edit I Name Create
A1	NAME
A2	ADD1
A3	ADD2
A4	TEL

Once the structure of formulae has been written and tested with some sample values, the rows containing these values can be deleted and customer details erased. The emptied sheet can then be saved as CUSTBASE, or something similar, and will serve as a template for the individual worksheets for the customers.

Changeable links

Now, we have a problem in trying to draw the customer's details into the invoicing sheet, as those details will be written on umpteen different sheets. We could avoid the problem altogether and use **Edit I Copy** to collect the details 'by hand'. Alternatively, we could write a set of linking references now, and update the links to point to the relevant sheet when we begin work on an invoice. Let's do that.

The cells that take the customer's details on the invoice sheet could have their initial links made to the CUSTBASE sheet:

```
E3:  +[CUSTBASE]NAME
E4:  +[CUSTBASE]ADD1
etc.
```

When the stock list and invoicing sheets are loaded *without their supporting sheet*, these cells will display NA messages – but not for long. The invoicing clerk will next open the sheet for the specific customer and update the links to point to that. Assume that the sheet was called FISSION (for the well-known 'Fission Chip' shop). This sequence would update the links:

1 From the **Tools** menu, select **Update Links**.

2 A small window appears displaying the names of linked sheets. From this select CUSTBASE – the one used in the initial references.

3 When prompted for the name of the new sheet, enter 'FISSION'.

All references that had previously linked to CUSTBASE will now link to FISSION.

Can the clerk cope?

Will the person doing the invoices be able to cope with the commands to make the system work? And even if he/she could, wouldn't it be better if the job could be simplified? Of course it would be better to make it easier to use, and fortunately, that is something that can be arranged without too much trouble. All it takes is a few macros.

PART EIGHT

Macros

■ SECTION 38
Macros save time

In the early days of spreadsheeting, macros were not much more than keyboard shortcuts – packing a simple sequence of commands into a single keystroke. They can still serve that purpose, but nowadays macros can do much more than that. In Quattro Pro, as in other leading spreadsheets, the macro system has been extended to the point where it is a programming language. If you care to take the time and effort, you can use the macro facilities to create menu-driven spreadsheet applications that are so tightly structured and crash-proofed that the temp could use them on the first day in the office. A full exploration of macro programming is not within the scope of this book, but in the next few sections we will look at ways of automating routine chores and of building simple menu-driven programs.

So what exactly is a macro? In essence it is a written sequence of commands that, when executed, replicates the work that you would do, sitting at the keyboard. This includes not simply the command and movement keystrokes, but also some of the decisions that you would make. A macro might load or save files, move to a different cell or window, send a sheet for printing, copy a block of data, check results and alert you to problems.

An @SUM macro
Here are a few typical macros. First, one that reproduces the series of characters and cursor movements that write an @SUM formula.

```
@sum({UP}.{END}{UP})~
```

When this macro is executed, the start of the function @SUM(will appear in the entry line; {UP} and {END}{UP} are equivalent to pressing the [Up] arrow and [End] keys and will define the block above the cell; the end bracket then falls into place and the tilde ~ is the [RETURN] press that transfers the formula into the cell. On a sheet like that in Figure 38.1, if you executed the macro with

198

■ SECTION 38
Macros save time

the cursor on A7, it would write the formula @SUM(A1..A6) into that cell.

	A	B	C	D	E
1	12	18	16	12	
2	19	18	10	10	
3	16	19	11	18	
4	10	12	15	13	
5	11	14	14	11	
6	14	13	12	18	
7					

Figure 38.1

Copying a formula

The second example calls up the **Edit I Copy** command and copies a formula – perhaps that @SUM – across the bottom of a table. In Figure 38.1, this could be used to copy the new formula in A7, across from B7 to D7.

```
{/ Block;Copy}~.{UP}{END}{RIGHT}{DOWN}~
```

Here the keystroke sequence /EC – **/E**dit I **Copy** – has been translated into {/ Block;Copy}. This is the *logical* macro equivalent, a form which is generally easier to read. Macros can be written in the more succinct but less readable *keystroke* mode. This one would then appear as:

```
/EC~.{UP}{END}{RIGHT}{DOWN}~
```

What does the rest of the sequence do?

■ SECTION 38
Macros save time

Printing the active area

Macros are not restricted to a single operation. The next one does all that is necessary to give you a quick printout of the active area of the sheet.

```
{/ Print;Block}
{HOME}.{END}{HOME}~
{/ Print;OutputPrinter}
{/ Print;Go}~
```

Notice that the first job, selecting the **Print I Block** option and defining the area to print, has been split over two lines. This doesn't matter. The system simply works down the column of cells until it runs out of things to do. A cell can contain a whole macro, a part of one, or a string of several – it's the sequence of commands and keystrokes that counts, not the layout.

Spend a little time exploring macros, and – even if you don't fell inclined to try full-blown macro programs – at least create simple ones to automate routine chores.

■ SECTION 39
Writing and executing macros

Macros can be created by writing the commands and keywords as labels directly into the spreadsheet – and you will have to do this with the more complex ones. But the simpler keystroke macros can be created faster and more conveniently by using the facilities on the Macro menu.

The Macro menu
Pull this into view by selecting **Tools|Macro**, or by pressing [Alt]-[F2]. There are ten options, of which four are important at this stage:

■ **Record** is an **On/Off** toggle. Switch the Record On, and all subsequent keystrokes will be stored in memory, ready for later use as a macro. When you have captured the sequence, either switch Record Off, or go straight to ...

■ **Paste**. This allows you to transfer the recorded keystrokes onto on open spreadsheet, where they will appear as a column of labels. The block where they are to be written must have a name – create it at the time or re-use an old one – but don't worry too much about the size. Just give the first cell and make sure that there is plenty of free space beneath it – the macro will overwrite any occupied cells.

An important point to note about recorded macros is that the process does not appear to be 100 per cent reliable (not at least in version 3.0). Always test them thoroughly before using them in earnest.

■ **Execute** is one way of running a macro. It asks for the name, then runs through the sequence of commands that start at the named cell. Execution stops when the system reaches a blank cell, or when it hits a problem. As the commands rattle through at a great rate of knots, it's all but impossible to spot what's happening. So if there are problems, you will have to turn to ...

■ **Debugger**. This is another **On/Off** toggle. When it is on, the DEBUG mode indicator shows down in the bottom line. When you execute a macro, it is displayed in the bottom quarter of the screen, with a highlight on the current command or keystroke. The commands and keystrokes are performed one at a time as you press the space bar, making it much simpler to track down the source of the error.

Keystroke execution

If you name the first cell of a macro with \ followed by a single letter, you can execute it by pressing [Alt] and the letter. So, a macro named \P (perhaps for Print) could be run with the keystroke [Alt]-[P]. Try to stick to initials – they're easier to remember.

There's a special case, related to these. If you name a macro \0, it will run automatically when the sheet is loaded into memory. Auto-run a user-friendly controlling macro progam, and you have a sheet that can be handled by anyone.

Automated worksheets

Back in Section 37, we developed a simple invoicing system which included a sheet containing a stock list. With a little enlargement and the addition of a macro, this can be upgraded into a stock control sheet.

The sheet will be updated by recording the movements of stock Out and In (columns E and F, Figure 40.1). These will be combined with the Opening stock to give the Closing stock. The (retail) Value can be usefully included.

```
G4:  +D4-E4+F4    {Closing = Opening - Out + In}
H4:  +G4*C4       {Value   = Closing * Price}
```

This sounds straightforward, but on a spreadsheet it requires a bit of management. At the start of a session you have to copy the values from Closing to Opening (with Edit I Value) and erase all

	A	B	C	D	E	F	G	H
1	Stock List							
2								
3	Code	Type	Price	Opening	Out	In	Closing	Value
4	1	Large Cod	£2.45	200	100	100	200	£490.00
5	2	Small Cod	£2.37	150	75		75	£177.75
6	3	Haddock	£2.67	160	100	125	185	£493.95
7	4	Smoked Ha	£4.30	0		200	200	£860.00
8	5	Coley	£1.15	120	90	100	130	£149.50
9	6	Mackerel	£2.79	240	240	300	300	£837.00
10	7	Shrimps	£3.90	50	45	25	30	£117.00
11	8	Lobster	£4.65	12	9	10	13	£60.45
12	9	Crab	£3.60	28	25	20	23	£82.80
13	10	Mussels	2.75	90	0	0	90	£247.50
14								
15								£3,373.15
16								

Figure 40.1

the Out and In figures. It's a chore, but with macros you will only have to do it once.

Run up a sample sheet along the lines of Figure 40.1, or adapt your stock worksheet to give the same structure, then follow through these steps.

A word of caution! Any errors – and their corrections – that you make while creating the macro will be repeated each time the macro is run. So, save the sheet before you start and, if an error occurs, stop recording. If the sheet has been changed, retrieve the earlier version before starting again.

1 Call up the macro menu and turn **Record On**.

2 Press [F5] – GoTo – and enter G4 (or whatever cell is at the top of your Closing column). Do not move to the cell with the cursor keys or mouse. If you do, then the macro will only work if you happen to be on the same starting cell next time!

3 Use the **Edit I Value** command to copy the Closing values across to the Opening column.

4 Go to the top of the Out column – you can move the cursor this time, if you like.

5 Give the **Edit I Erase** command to clear the Out and In block.

6 Call up the macro menu and select **Paste**.

7 Press [Escape] to release the cursor – the system assumes that you want to paste where you are. Move to a convenient blank space to the right or below the working area, and select that as the macro area.

8 Give it the name \U (for Update). You should find that this macro has been written into the sheet.

{GOTO}G4~	GoTo the top of Closing
{/ Block;Values}	/Edit|Values
{DOWN 9}~	Copy from the G column
{LEFT 3}~	Across to D
{LEFT 2}	Move to the top of Out.
{/ Block;Erase}	/Edit|Erase
{RIGHT}	Across to In ..
{DOWN 9}~	.. and down the column

At the start of the next session, just press [Alt]-[U] and the copying and clearing will be done for you.

Macros across sheets

In this second example, we'll automate another chore in the invoicing system. The customer's worksheet is designed to be expanded row by row as invoices are added. This involves inserting a new row, copying the formulae up from the (permanent) versions in the lowest row of the table, copying the invoice number across from the INBASE sheet, and finally fixing the values after they have been drawn in from INBASE. The latter move is essential, for if left as formulae, these would pull in new values each time the INBASE invoice sheet was re-used.

A key problem that must be solved here is, where do you insert a new row? When you are working directly with the sheet, the answer is visibly obvious. For example, in Figure 40.2, the next

```
        A          B        C        D        E        F        G
1   Fission Chips
2   Seaview St
3   Cleethorpes
4   0472 654321
5
6   Credit Limit      500
7
8   Inv. No.    Date      Total    Pay Date Amount   Due      Age of Debt
9   915432      13/02/91   413.65 28/01/91   413.65    0.00
10  915435      13/03/91   181.15 04/03/91   181.15    0.00
11  92342       02/05/91   178.25                    178.25        34
12                                                      0.00
13                         773.05            594.8   178.25
14
```

Figure 40.2

row will fit between rows 11 (the last used one) and 12 (which holds the formulae copies). As the macro interpreter cannot 'see' the sheet, we must give it something more tangible to work with. The solution is to name the cell in the first column of the lower row. Here, A12 is named NEXT. If we go to this cell and insert a row, it will be in the right place and the NEXT row will pushed down ready for next time.

The formulae that are to be copied up from the lower row are given here for reference:

```
B12:  @IF(A12>"",[INBASE]$DATE,"")
                              - Note $Absolute reference
C12:  @IF($A12>"",[INBASE]$TOTAL,"")
D12:   blank, formatted as a Date
E12:   blank, formatted as Fixed, 2
F12:  +C12-E12
G12:  @IF(A12>"",@TODAY-D12,"")
```

■ SECTION 40
Automated worksheets

The macro is best created by recording the process as you work through it by hand. It should look like this:

```
{GOTO}next~              - do use GoTo
{/ Row;Insert}~          - insert a row above
{DOWN}                   - down to the formulae row
{/ Block;Copy}{RIGHT 6}~{UP}~
                         - copy A..G up a row
{UP}                     - up to start of new row
{/ Block;Copy}[inbase]invno~~
                         - copy inv. no. from INBASE
{/ Block;Values}{RIGHT 2}~~
                         - fix Date & Total as values
```

The macro should be pasted into the INBASE sheet – not the account sheet, as each customer has a separate version of this. To be executed, a macro does not have to be on the current sheet, as long as it is present somewhere in memory.

■ SECTION 41
Macro programming

The Quattro Pro macro programming language has a vocabulary of over 100 words, giving extensive control over the keyboard, screen, disk files, interaction with the user and the operations of the macros themselves. It is therefore not possible to do more than give a flavour of macro programming in a book of this size. Those of you who have previously written programs in other macro systems, or in other computer languages, should have little difficulty in transferring your experience to Quattro. If you are a newcomer to programming, Quattro macros are a good a place to start as any – and better than most.

You can get the flavour of macro programming – and create some handy little programs – just using a small sub-set of the commands. Note that commands are written here in capitals to make them stand out, but lower case will do.

Interaction with the user

{GETLABEL *prompt, cell*} displays a prompt in the entry line and waits for something to be typed in. This is then transferred – as a label – to the given cell. The prompt must be written in double quotes. For example:

```
{GETLABEL "Please enter name:",CLIENT}
{GETLABEL "Telephone No:",TELNO}
```

Though the telephone number will be entered in digits, it will be treated as a string – as phone numbers should be.

{GETNUMBER *prompt, cell*} is the same as GETLABEL, but for numbers. If text is entered, it will be treated as an error and the command will be repeated.

{?} hands over control to the user for one operation. It may be for free data entry – as opposed to the tightly controlled entry of the

{GET...} commands – or to perform a command. Once [Return] is pressed, the macro carries on from the next line. Note that this only works for a single operation. If the user needs control of the keyboard for an indefinite period, the simplest solution us to end the macro and get the user to restart it. Which is where the next command may come in.

{**MESSAGE** block, character column, row, delay} displays a message on the screen, with the top left corner at the given location, for a time of delay seconds. The block can be as large as you like – within the limits of the screen, but must be wide enough to display the cell contents in full. Long labels will not overflow a message block as they will a normal cell. If the delay is set to 0, the message remains visible until a key is pressed.

Suppose you want to remind the user how to restart the macro, with the message:

```
Press [Alt]-[M]
To Restart Macro
```

This could be written off-screen, perhaps at Z1 and Z2. The Z column should be widened to 16 characters, so the text fits, and the block Z1..Z2 named as RESTART. On an 80-character, 25-line screen, the block will be more or less central if it starts at column 30, row 10. With an indefinite delay, that gives us:

```
{MESSAGE restart,30,10,0}
```

{**GRAPHCHAR** cell} is used solely to collect the keypress after a MESSAGE (or graph) display. The character will be stored in the given cell.

■ SECTION 41
Macro programming

Program flow

{**BRANCH** *cell*} takes the flow of the program to the given cell and picks up the execution from there. It is always best to use a *named* cell, not a reference; references in macros are not adjusted – as they are in formulae – during Insert/Delete/Move operations.

{**IF** *test*} *do-if-true* allows you to build decision-making into your macros. The tests are the same as in the @IF function, comparing cell contents against given values or other cells. If the result is true, the interpreter will execute the command(s) in the rest of the line, before moving on to the next cell. If the next command is a BRANCH, then the flow will go elsewhere on the sheet if the test is true, and only reach the next cell if it is false. You might, for instance, want to include a check before quitting a macro system:

```
{MESSAGE check,20,5,0}   Check says 'Really Quit (Y/N)'
{GRAPHCHAR temp}
{IF temp="Y"} {QUIT}     {QUIT} exits from macro
{BRANCH restart}
```

{**MENUBRANCH** *cell*} is a kind of BRANCH instruction, in that it takes the flow to a different cell. More importantly, it activates a macro **menu**. In use, these are much the same as normal menus. The list of possible options appears in a small window; the Help line will show a reminder about whichever is highlighted; and selection is by mouse-click, [Return] or the option's initial. (So make sure they all start with a different letter!)

The menu layout must follow a fixed pattern. Options must be written in adjacent columns – a blank right-hand column indicates the end of the menu; and each will occupy at least three rows. The first row contains the name, the second has the Help line entry but can be left blank; and the third is the first line of the macro routine for that option. In Figure 41.1, you will see a menu with four options. In the first three cases, selection leads to a single BRANCH command (we can assume that SUM, COPY and PRINT are the first cells of three macros); in the last, an exit-check routine is written directly into the menu lines. It is a bit different from the one we looked at earlier – which just goes to show that there is always more than one way to tackle any programming task. {/ System;TidyUp} is the logical equivalent of File | Close.

To activate the menu, you must have a {MENUBRANCH ...} to the cell in the top left corner of the layout. In this case, it is the cell containing the label Sum (A42), which has been named MAIN. The {MENUBRANCH ...} is just a normal command, and could be one part of a longer macro or stand-alone, as here. It does not need to be attached to the menu in any way.

```
        A              B              C              D
40
41   {MENUBRANCH MAIN}
42   Sum            Copy                Printout      Quit
43   Sum a column Copy across a row Print the sheet Close and Exit
44   {BRANCH SUM}  {BRANCH COPY}      {BRANCH PRINT} {GETLABEL "Really?",A50}
                                                     {IF A50="N"}{MENUBRANCH MAIN}
                                                     {/ System;TidyUp}
```

Figure 41.1

A sample system

Finally, a small menu-driven macro system to automate some of the routine chores in the invoicing spreadsheet. The menu has four options, each of which leads to a {BRANCH ...} command to leap to the appropriate routine. The four small macros all have \ names as this allows them to be developed and run independently of the menu.

■SECTION 41
Macro programming

The menu has been named `menu` – why not? – and its {MENU-BRANCH ...} activator is called `\M`. Pressing [Alt]-[M] will get the system running.

```
{MENUBRANCH menu}
Start            Print            File             Quit
Get data         Print Invoice    Save Invoice     Close and Exit
{BRANCH \s}~     {BRANCH \p}      {BRANCH \f}~     {BRANCH \c}
```

The **Start** routine asks for the invoice number, and stores that in the right cell – as a label. (The reason for this will be clear when you look at the next option.) It then moves to the beginning of the data entry area – named `code` – and displays a message to remind the user to restart the macro with [Alt]-[M]. The message block should be named `mess1`.

```
\s start
{GETLABEL "Invoice No. ",invno}      mess1 block
{GOTO}code~                          [Alt]-[M]
{MESSAGE mess1,30,10,0}              When done
```

Print Invoice follows the same pattern as in the earlier example. It only prints the active part of the sheet – the customers will not want macros scattered over their invoices – and this block should be named `printer`. After printing, it returns to the startup cell and thence to the main menu. That last line could equally well have been {MENUBRANCH menu}.

```
\p Print Invoice
{/ Print;Block}printer~
{/ Print;OutputHQ}
{/ Print;Go}
{BRANCH \m}
```

212

SECTION 41
Macro programming

The File routine introduces a new idea – macros that write themselves! It needs a line that will create a suitable filename from the invoice number. Invoice 91234, for example, we would want to save as IN91234.WQ1. This is the line that does the trick:

```
"{/ File;ExtractFormulas}in" & INVNO & "~printer~"
```

Notice that the first and last parts of the command are written in quotes, which they would not normally be. Between them, and joining them with ampersands (&), is the INVNO cell reference. This will collect the invoice number as a label, and the ampersands tie the whole lot together to make a single string. This is what the macro interpreter sees, and it executes it just as if it had been written in the usual way. The example here was taken from a sheet where the invoice number was 92342.

```
\f Save File
{/ File;ExtractFormulas}in92342~printer~
{BRANCH \m}
```

For the Close and Exit, you need a second message block – named mess2 – and a cell to store a reply, named answer. If the user changes his mind about quitting, the routine jumps back to the start. If not, it closes down the worksheets and exits from the system.

```
\c Close and Exit                     Message Two
{MESSAGE mess2,30,10,0}               Really Quit?
{GRAPHCHAR answer}                    Yes/No
{IF @UPPER(answer)="N"}{BRANCH \m}
{/ System;TidyUp}
```

■ SECTION 41
Macro programming

It should be obvious that macros can save quite a bit of time, by simplifying routine operations. Once you start macro programming you will also discover that they can waste a lot of time. All programming is addictive. It is a fascinating intellectual challenge to devise a neat solution to a problem, and people can get quite obsessive tracking down the bugs that are making nonsense of their beautiful design. I'm sure I'm not the only one to have spent more time developing a macro to do a job than it would have taken me to do it by hand. But it was great to watch it run!

PART NINE

Data management

■ SECTION 42
Data and databases

Databases are among the most common business computing applications, for computerised files can be so much more efficient than paper-based ones. They take far less time to maintain and use. New entries can be quickly slotted into the right place – for the computer will do any sorting that may be required – and updating old records is simply a matter of getting the computer to find the ones you want then typing in the new data. A single file can be produce lists organised in different ways to suit different purposes – alphabetical by name, by rank order of values, grouped by town, type or whatever. The data from multiple files can be cross-referenced to get combined reports; you might, for example, link the customer name and address file with the sales order file to output statements and invoices.

Quattro Pro's data-management facilities allow you to use the spreadsheet as a database, i.e. for the storage and retrieval of information of any kind. It could be used in place of a simple card index system, for storing addresses or similar reference material; but the data-management facilities may also be combined with the normal calculation functions to provide a very useful tool. The simple stock control system outlined here should give some idea of what can be achieved by combining these aspects of the software.

In any database, information is organised into files, records and fields. A file is a collection of related data – names and addresses, stock or employees' details – which in a card index system would be kept in one box, and in Quattro would have its own spreadsheet.

A record can be thought of as a card in a card index system. It holds the information about one individual, company, product or whatever. The record is subdivided into fields, as the card is marked out into areas or lines in which particular items must be written. In Quattro, each record occupies a whole row, and the cells are the fields. With a standard database package, you would have to define the nature and size of each field: is it a number, date or item of text, and how many characters or digits will there be? This is not necessary with Quattro. Whether used for database or normal spreadsheet purposes, a cell will stretch to fit anything that is written in it. Of course, if the database is to be used properly, the equivalent field in every record – the ones in the same column – should hold the same type of data.

There are some things that Quattro-the-Database does not do very well. It is, for instance, useless at mailing labels and poor at personalised circulars. Where the record occupies more than a screen width, there is no simple way to view the record as a whole, and there are other limitations that appear as you start to expand its uses. However, the database functions are quite adequate for the central data processing chores, and if more is needed, data can pass seamlessly from Quattro to Borland's Paradox.

Setting up a Quattro database

With any database, the first job is always to look closely at the data itself. What information do you wish to store? How is it to be arranged? What structure of fields is required? In this section, we will create a database of Databases – part of the stock control system for a computer software shop.

It is a simple system, fortunately, recording only the cost price, quantity in stock, stock value, selling price, total sales and sales value for each item. That gives us six fields, plus one for the name. These are written as headings across the top of the table in Figure 42.1. The records are then entered on the rows beneath.

This horizontal organisation is essential – the database routines will not work if you arrange the records into columns. The field names at the top of each column are also essential. These aren't

Data and databases

	A	B	C	D	E	F	G
1	Database Management						
2							
3			Stock			Sales	
4	Title	Cost	Qty	Value	Price	Total	Salesval
5	dBase III+	140	5	700	225	8	1800
6	DBase IV	245	10	2450	399	20	7980
7	Paradox	195	8	1560	349	35	12215
8	Clipper V5	225	6	1350	349	10	3490
9	Retrieve	60	2	120	95	3	285
10	Dataease	270	12	3240	395	18	7110
11	Foxbase	235	4	940	369	7	2583
12							
13				10360			35463
14							

Figure 42.1

just for your benefit – as they might be on a card index – but are vital to the operation of many of the data management functions. Database fields can hold numbers, labels or formulae. They are no different from any other cells, and it important to note is that the database may well occupy only part of the sheet. In the example, the block A4..G12 is the database. Other parts of the sheet can be used for related headings and calculations – as here – or for any other purposes.

You may like to type in this sample sheet, or a similar one using your own data, to give you something to work with as we explore the data-management facilities. Do make sure that every field name is unique – things won't work properly if you have two the same. Don't worry about the order in which you enter the records. One of the most attractive features of databases, as compared with paper filing systems, is that you don't have to bother about any kind of index order. The system can find records wherever they may be, and should you want an organised list, it can be produced in a matter of moments – and in the order that you choose.

■ SECTION 43
Locating records

To get information out of a database, you have to tell the system two, or three, things – where the data is, what it is you are looking for and, if you want a copy of the records, where to put them. In all cases, it is a matter of defining a block on the sheet. Let's start now with the database block.

1 Move to the start of the database – i.e. the first field heading, not the first record.

2 Pull down the **Data** menu and select **Query**.

3 From this menu, select **Block**.

4 Spread the highlight to include all the fields and at least one blank row below the last record. (In the sheet shown in Figure 43.1, this would be A4..G12.) If you want to add more records later, you can insert them above the bottom row and not have to redefine the block.

5 The **Query** menu remains active, in case you want to perform more data-management operations. We can't yet, so Quit.

We will return to the Data Query menu shortly, but first we must do a little more preparation.

Defining search criteria
There are two aspects to this – what you are looking for, and where to look for it. It may be the record where the Title is 'Paradox', those where the Price is less than £300 or those with a Cost of over £200 and with Total sales of more than 10.

Locating records

	A	B	C	D	E	F	G
1	Database Management						
2							
3			Stock			Sales	
4	Title	Cost	Qty	Value	Price	Total	Salesval
5	dBase III+	140	5	700	225	8	1800
6	DBase IV	245	10	2450	399	20	7980
7	Paradox	195	8	1560	349	35	12215
8	Clipper V5	225	6	1350	349	10	3490
9	Retrieve	60	2	120	95	3	285
10	Dataease	270	12	3240	395	18	7110
11	Foxbase	235	4	940	369	7	2583
12							
13				10360			35463
14	Criteria Table						
15	Title						
16	Paradox						

Figure 43.1

The information is written into a part of the sheet that will be defined as the **Criteria** table. At the simplest it consists of two cells in a column, containing the field name and the search criteria. For example:

```
Title      {Field name}
Paradox    {Item to search for}
```

Just writing this on the sheet is not enough, of course. You must tell the system about the table. Pull down the Data Query menu and select **Criteria Table**. Define it to include the field name and search item cells only. Stay on the menu – we want it again.

The Locate command
The **Data|Query Locate** command finds each record – if any – that matches the given criteria. It does so one record at a time, moving the cursor to the first field. At that point you can move

across the fields, editing entries as necessary. Moving up or down will take you to the next matching record. When you have done whatever editing or checking was needed, press [Escape] to exit from the Locate routine back to the Data Query menu.

Try it, then [Escape] again, or **Quit** to get back to the main screen. As we look at the different forms of criteria, you might like to test them out with Locate.

Looking for matches

When you are searching for a particular label or value, all you need to do is write in what you want – here it is 'Paradox'. Case is irrelevant. 'PARADOX' and 'paradox' will equally well find Paradox, if it is in there. In just the same way, we can find which databases we are selling at £349.

```
Price
   349
```

That will track down Paradox and Clipper in the example in Figure 43.1.

Wildcards

Wildcards can be used in label searches, much as in DOS commands, to replace one or more characters so that you can find groups of related items or those where you are unsure of the spelling.

? stands for any single character. To find a customer called Smith – or was it Smyth? – the criteria table would be:

```
Name
Sm?th
```

* will replace a group of letters. In the example database (Figure 43.1), the criteria `dBase*` would find both `dBase III+` and `DBase IV`. (And note that the irregular use of capitals was ignored.)

~ (tilde) is an 'everything but' signal. You might have an accounts database where invoices are marked with a 'P' when they are paid. To find those that have not been paid you might use:

```
Paid?
~P
```

Making comparisons
These are normally done on values, to find those items above or below certain limits, but will work with labels. Any comparison must be written as a formula, and one that would test the first cell in the relevant field. So, if you wanted to pick out the cheaper database systems – those with a price below £300 – the criteria table should be:

```
Price
+E5<300    {it will display 1, as this is true}
```

When the search operation is executed, it will start in the first cell below the Price heading (E5) and apply the test +E5<300 to it. It then moves down to the next cell and performs a +E6<300 test, and so on down the database.

A comparison search on labels takes much the same format. Characters are 'more than' or 'less than' others on the basis of their ASCII codes. Digits come before letters, but capitals are not distinguished from lower case. "e" and "E" are both greater than "D" and less than "F". If, for whatever reason, you wanted to pick out those databases with names beginning H or later, you would set up this criteria table:

```
Title
+A5>"G"     {always write the test on the first cell!}
```

That would find Paradox and Retrieve.

Multiple criteria

So far we have used only single criteria – setting one condition for one field – but you can test on two or more fields at once, or set several possible conditions for a field. Suppose you wanted to find which of the better-selling packages needed restocking. The criteria might be that the sales total is at least 20, and the quantity in stock no more than 10. The criteria table would be defined to cover the two-by-two block containing:

```
Qty         Total
+C5<=10     +F5>=20
```

This is an **AND** test. If the quantity is less than or equal to 10 AND the total more than or equal to 20, then a record passes the test.

In a customer database, you might want to track down those in East Anglia to make up a visiting list for your rep. The criteria table this time would be stretched down to include the alternative county entries:

```
County
Norfolk     {or use wildcards and replace these
Suffolk      two lines by a single ???folk}
Essex
```

Mind you, if you want a list, locating its entries one at a time will be a tedious process. Let's find a better way.

■ SECTION 44
Extracting and deleting records

Quattro's Extract command allows you to create a sub-set of records that meet given criteria. Rather than locate the matching records one by one, Extract copies the data from some or all of the fields of each record into an **Output** block – so let's see how to set one of those up.

In Figure 44.1, the Output block is located at A19..C24. It is headed, as is the data block, but only with the names of those fields that we are interested in at this stage. In the example, the user wanted a list of the cheaper databases – the criteria was E5<350 – and only needed the names, retail prices and quantity

	A	B	C	D	E	F	G
1	Database Management						
2							
3			Stock			Sales	
4	Title	Cost	Qty	Value	Price	Total	Salesval
5	dBase III+	140	5	700	225	8	1800
6	DBase IV	245	10	2450	399	20	7980
7	Paradox	195	8	1560	349	35	12215
8	Clipper V5	225	6	1350	349	10	3490
9	Retrieve	60	2	120	95	3	285
10	Dataease	270	12	3240	395	18	7110
11	Foxbase	235	4	940	369	7	2583
12							
13				10360			35463
14	Criteria Block						
15	Price						
16	1						
17							
18	Output Block...............						
19	Title	Price	Qty				
20	dBase III+	225	5				
21	Paradox	349	8				
22	Clipper V5	349	6				
23	Retrieve	95	2				
24							

Figure 44.1

224

Extracting and deleting records

in stock. In a customer accounts database, you might want to chase up slow payers, and a list containing names, telephone numbers, age of debt and amount owing would be sufficient.

Using Data I Query Extract

1 Decide where the output block will fit, and write into the first line the names of the fields that you want to include.

2 Set up the Criteria table to specify the records you want.

3 Activate the **Data Query** menu.

4 Select **Output** and define a block that starts with the headings and stretches down far enough to give space for all the records that may be extracted. If you don't have a clue how many records may match the criteria, make the extract block as deep as the database itself. There's no harm in making it too big, but if it is too small, the Extract routine will complain about it.

5 Select **Extract**, wait for a moment, then **Quit**.

6 Move down to the Output block and see what you have got. If you want a hard copy of the list, then Print it.

Although this is called **Extract**, it doesn't actually remove records from the data block, merely copies of them. If you really want to remove records, you must *delete* them.

■ SECTION 44
Extracting and deleting records

Deleting records

Delete is the other key data-management command that uses criteria. When given, it removes matching records from the database and closes up the gaps, creating a set of blank rows at the bottom. [Alt]-[F5] – Undo – will put them back if the operation was a mistake, but it is always best to use this with care. Hard-won data should not be lightly thrown away. It is a good idea to perform an Extract first, and check that the criteria really are getting the records you want to delete – and only those!

■ SECTION 45
Sorting into order

The data-management commands are perfectly happy working with unsorted records, but there are times when you will want to get a database into order for your own purposes. You may want an alphabetical list of customers by name or town, or stock sorted by sales value, with the best-sellers at the top.

The **Data Sort** command will sort into order a block of data on the basis of one or more key columns, and sort alphabetically or by value, in ascending or descending order. It also does it remarkably quickly! On a moderately fast PC AT, for instance, it can sort over 1,000 records into order in a little over five seconds.

The records in our example database have been entered in a piecemeal fashion and could well be sorted. The question is, into which order? To sort it by title, we would use this sequence:

1 Pull down the **Data** menu and thence the **Sort** sub-menu.

2 Select **Block** and define the area A5..G12, to include all the data, but not the headings.

3 Select **1st Key**, move the cursor to any cell in column A and press [Return].

4 Select **Sort Order**, either **A** (Ascending) or **D** (Descending).

5 Select **Go** to run the sort, then **Quit** to return to the main screen.

The result of this sort is shown in Figure 45.1. Notice that the sort is case-sensitive, unlike the Data Query commands. dBase III+,

Sorting into order

	A	B	C	D	E	F	G
1	Database Management						
2							
3			Stock			Sales	
4	Title	Cost	Qty	Value	Price	Total	Salesval
5	Clipper V5	225	6	1350	349	10	3490
6	DBase IV	245	10	2450	399	20	7980
7	Dataease	270	12	3240	395	18	7110
8	Foxbase	235	4	940	369	7	2583
9	Paradox	195	8	1560	349	35	12215
10	Retrieve	60	2	120	95	3	285
11	dBase III+	140	5	700	225	8	1800
12							
13				10360			35463
14							

Figure 45.1

	A	B	C	D	E	F	G
1	Database Management						
2							
3			Stock			Sales	
4	Title	Cost	Qty	Value	Price	Total	Salesval
5	DBase IV	245	10	2450	399	20	7980
6	Dataease	270	12	3240	395	18	7110
7	Foxbase	235	4	940	369	7	2583
8	Paradox	195	8	1560	349	35	12215
9	Clipper V5	225	6	1350	349	10	3490
10	dBase III+	140	5	700	225	8	1800
11	Retrieve	60	2	120	95	3	285
12							
13				10360			35463
14							
15							

Figure 45.2

■ SECTION 45
Sorting into order

with its lower-case 'd', has been placed after those that started with capitals.

In Figure 45.2, the data block has been sorted again. This time, column E was selected as the 1st Key, and the order set to Descending.

■ SECTION 46
Quattro Pro and Paradox

Though the Quattro Pro data-management facilities are easy to handle and quick and efficient in operation, they are distinctly limited. Any reports from the database must inevitably be tabular: one record to a row, which rules out producing mailshot circulars, or even mailing labels from your Quattro database. Relational database work – cross-referencing between files – is also all but impossible, though data can be copied and cross-checked by hand between sheets in a multi-window system.

I suppose it would just be possible to write a macro that would transfer data one field at a time to a separate part of the sheet, drop it into the appropriate slot in a circular or label layout, print that block then return for the next record. Likewise you could, in theory, produce a macro that would perform relational operations – but in either case it would be an awful chore, and fraught with opportunities for error!

So, when you need to do any database work that goes beyond the basic locate, extract and sort operations, it's time to reach for a full-blown database management system. And the obvious choice for Quattro users is Borland's Paradox. The two are designed to be used with each other, and if your computer has sufficient memory – preferably at least 2MB – the two can be resident simultaneously, with hot-key switching between them. If not, then passing files between the two is easily done.

Quattro Pro to Paradox

Paradox will happily import files from Quattro Pro in worksheet format, checking each column of data to see what size and type of field it should become. A little prior work may be needed before the file leaves Quattro, if it is to work properly. The problem is that Paradox assumes that the first row in the worksheet is the one containing the field names, and all the remaining rows are records. As 'database' worksheets will normally also have criteria tables,

230

■SECTION 46
Quattro Pro and Paradox

output blocks, summary calculations, assorted headings and other extraneous materials, even these cannot be imported directly into Paradox.

The solution is simple enough. Quattro has on its **Tools** menu an **Extract** command, which will save part of a worksheet as a separate file. It has two options: **Formulae** and **Values**. The first would be used if the extracted block was to be used as an independent worksheet; where the file is to be passed across to Paradox, take the [b]Values[r] option. The block to be extracted will, of course, be the database, from the headings down to the last record.

Like the **Data|Query Extract**, the **Tools|Extract** does not remove the original data. It just takes a copy.

There should be no problems at the Paradox end of the transfer. The system has extensive Import facilities, and can take files from many sources. Just select the Quattro Pro mode, give it the name of the (extracted) file and leave it to its own devices. (You may need to change directories first, or include the directory path in the filename.)

Paradox to Quattro Pro
This is even easier. From the Paradox end, just select the Quattro Pro Export mode, and give a suitable filename – with directory path if necessary. What happens when you get back into Quattro Pro, depends upon how you want to use the file.

You can simply retrieve the file in the normal way – but note that all you will have will be the headings and records of the database. If you want to do more data-management work within Quattro, you will then have to add a Criteria table and Output area, and define the blocks on the Data Query menu.

■ SECTION 46
Quattro Pro and Paradox

If the file had been originally extracted from a database worksheet, and you want to put it back into place – presumably because it was edited while in Paradox, as you wouldn't bother otherwise – then you will have to go back to the **Tools** menu. There you will find a command called **Combine**. This allows you to merge data from another sheet into the current one. The merge can be an overwriting **Copy**, or can **Add** or **Subtract** the values of the equivalent file and current cells.

To combine an extracted and Paradox-processed file back into a database worksheet, you would go through these steps:

1 Move the cursor to the top left corner of your database area – this is where the combined sheet will be inserted, and you must do it now. You will have no opportunity to sort out position afterwards.

2 Call up the **Tools** menu and select **Combine**.

3 Select **Copy**, so that the new data overwrites the existing cell contents.

4 Select **File** and give the name of the worksheet to be inserted.

PART TEN

Annotated graphs & presentations

The Annotator is such a comprehensive piece of software that I feel I should be writing a book about it, not just a couple of short chapters. Except that, like most modern software, its operation is largely intuitive, and once you've learned how to intuite, the rest follows easily – most of the time!

Its name understates its capabilities. Yes, you can use it to annotate a graph, but you can also draw your own diagrams and paste in clip-art pictures. A particularly sophisticated feature is that you can add *buttons*, which when selected will call up another graph, creating multi-branched structures of images. In all, Quattro Pro has many of the facilities that you would expect to find in a purpose-built presentation graphics package, but fully integrated with the spreadsheeting system.

Although the Annotator only works with graphs, there is a 'cheat mode' that lets you use it on a blank screen – handy for testing out techniques, but really intended for Title screens and text pages in presentations. If you want a blank screen, set up a new graph and select the **Text** Graph Type. Whether you have done this, or are working with an actual graph, get into the Annotator by pulling down the **Graph** menu and selecting **Annotate**. Do it now, and play with the system while you work through this section. It's the best way to learn.

The Annotator screen

The screen is split into five distinct parts:

■ The **Toolbox**, in the top line, displays the various tools at your disposal for creating and manipulating the image (see below).

■ The **Draw Area** is where the image is constructed. It is not a single whole image, such as you would have with an art package or drawing with pencil on paper. Instead it is composed of *elements* – each item on screen is treated individually.

■ The **Property Area** shows the properties of the current element or tool, such as line thickness, colour or font. These vary with the nature of the tool or element, and can be set before an element is created, or changed afterwards.

■ The **Gallery** displays the options available for the current property: the range of colours, patterns, line styles or whatever.

■ The **Status Box**, along the bottom of the screen, serves to remind you of what you are doing and what you can do next.

Elements
These include the background and the graph itself, its title and legend, as well as any text, drawings or clip pictures that you may have added. Elements can be selected individually or in groups to be moved, resized, recoloured, copied and deleted. When an element is selected, *handles* – little black squares – appear on its corners and sides. These serve as handy reminders, but more importantly are used for resizing the element.

The basic elements of the graph have somewhat different *properties* than added elements. Those of the background should be noted at an early stage.

The **Background Properties** are:

Background Button   Makes the whole background act as a button (see Section 48).

Grid Increment	There is an optional grid of dots which can help to position elements on the screen. It is initially set to 4% steps, giving 25 across, but can be set from a very fine grid of 1%, up to 25% – 4 dots across.
Grid Visible	Toggle between On and Off.
Grid Snap-to	When on, the corners of drawn elements will automatically go to the nearest point on the grid.

The Tools

The letter beside each name is the one to press if working from the keyboard.

■ **Pick** [P] to begin selecting elements.

■ **Clipboard** [C]: an element can be cut or copied from the screen and stored in memory, then be pasted back elsewhere later. Use Copy wherever you want identical or similar elements – it is quicker to change the size or style than to start from scratch. Your better efforts can also be saved (cut or copied) as files and loaded back into later graphs. The clip-art (.CLP) files that come with the Quattro package can also be pasted into graphs. Some of them are quite handy, and many are very clever. All are initially large and plain black and white, but can be resized or recoloured at will.

Priority is also controlled from the Clipboard. Select **Top** or **Bottom** where you have overlapping elements, to determine which is on top.

SECTION 47
The Annotator

■ **Text** [T]: in a range of fonts, sizes and colours, with optional background boxes. Text elements can only be resized by selecting them and changing the font size.

■ **Drawing Tools**: note that there is no 'eraser' in the set. If you make a mistake while drawing, [Escape] and start again. If you want to remove a completed drawing, select it and then press [Delete].

Arrow	– A
Single Line	– L
Multiple line	– Y
Polygon	– F
Rectangle	– R
Rounded Rectangle	– Z
Circle	– E
Vertical/Horizontal Line	– U

■ **Link** [X]: if an element is linked to a point on the graph, it will be moved up or down the image should the point's value change in the spreadsheet. To link an element, first select it, then specify which series and the **Link Index** – count the points from the left.

■ **Help** [F1]: as usual.

■ **Quit**. Now save the annotated graph with **Graph I Name Create**. This is especially important if the graph contains buttons to call up other graphs. If you View before you Save, you are liable to lose your graph.

■ SECTION 47
The Annotator

Working intuitively

There are certain ways of working that apply, with only minor variations, in all aspects of the system. It is easier with a mouse, but can be done adequately from the keyboard.

Mouse control

There are three basic operations:

Click	A single press on the left button
Double click	Press twice in quick succession
Drag	Hold down the button while moving the mouse

For any kind of selection: point and click. This applies whether you are selecting a tool, a property or an option from the gallery. Element selection is slightly different. Click first on **Pick**, then:

■ For a single element, click anywhere within it

■ For a group, enclose it by clicking on one corner and dragging a box to the opposite corner

■ For several scattered elements, hold down [Shift] and click each in turn

Drawing single lines, rectangles and circles: click at the starting point and drag to set the length or size.

Drawing multi-line elements: click and drag each line or side in turn, and double click to finish.

Moving an element: select it, then point within its space and drag the outline box to the new position.

Resizing an element: select it, then point to a handle and drag it. The outline box will expand or contract to indicate the new size.

Keyboard control

To select a tool: press [/] then use the [Left] or [Right] cursor keys to move across the Toolbox to the one you want, or use the Key letters. (See *The Tools*, above.)

To move between the Property and the Draw area: press [F3] to go to Property and [Escape] back to Draw.

To select an element: if in the Draw area, select **Pick** first, then press [Tab] or [Shift]-[Tab] to cycle forwards or backwards through the elements. The black box handles will indicate the current one.

To select more than one element: start as before, then press [Shift]-[F7] as you reach each desired element.

Drawing single lines, rectangles and circles: use the arrow keys to move the cross-hair cursor about the screen. For faster movement, hold down [Shift] and the cursor will leap from point to point on the grid (whether it is visible or not). Press [.] at the starting point, move to set the length or size, then press [Enter].

Drawing multi-line elements: press[.] to start and [Return] to end each line, then double [Return] to finish.

Moving an element: select it, then use the arrow keys to drag the outline box to the new position.

■ SECTION 47
The Annotator

Resizing an element: select it, then press [.]. A handle will appear on the bottom right corner only. Press [.] again to move this clockwise round to the most convenient corner, then use the arrow keys to shrink or expand the outline box.

As with all forms of desk-top publishing, the temptation is to make full use of all the facilities simply because they are there. Don't. Keep it simple and clearly focussed. That way you will get your message across with maximum impact. And if you have a lot of things to say, don't cram them onto one screen, make yourself a slideshow.

■ SECTION 48
Making a slideshow

Quattro offers two ways of creating sets of graphs for presentation purposes. You can set up a straightforward sequence with the **Graph I Name Slide** command, or produce a button-controlled system with the Annotator.

Slide sequences

A plain, no-frills sequence of graphs can be set up in a matter of moments. Write a list of graph names in the order that they are to appear:

```
BUDGET92
DEPTA
DEPTB
DEBTS
```

Then give the command **Graph I Name Slide** and highlight the block containing the list. That's it. The system will display each graph in turn and wait for a keypress before going on to the next.

Hands-off presentations

If you want your slideshow to run by itself, add a time column to the list of graph names, and set the number of seconds for which each will be displayed. When you give the Slide command, extend the highlight area to include the time column.

```
Graph Names      Seconds
BUDGET92         15
DEPTA            10
DEPTB            10
DEBTS            2
```

For exhibition or advertising purposes, you may want a presentation that cycles round through a series of screens. No problem with Quattro! Create your attractive screens with the Annotator, using text graphs for titles, diagrams and text pages. Set up the display sequence and timing, then write a little macro to keep repeating the Slide command.

```
{/ Graph;NameSlide}exhibit~
{BRANCH slideshow}
```

This assumes the slide block is named `exhibit`, and the first line of the macro is `slideshow`.

Visual effects

With an EGA or VGA monitor, you can have special transitions from one graph to the next, rather than the simple replacement of the screen. There are 24 possibilities, and with most you can set the speed of the effect. The speed number is not based on any constant value, but higher means slower.

No.	Speeds	
1	N/A	Cut – instant replace
2	0-any	Blackout before next screen
3-6	0-16	Wipes – right / left / up / down
7-8	0-16	Vertical split and close / open
9-10	0-16	Horizontal split and close / open
11-12	0-16	Camera iris close / open
13-14	0-16	Scroll up / down
15-16	0-16	Vertical stripes right / left
17	0-16	Spiral into centre
18-24	0-varies	Dissolves – from 2x1 to 64x64 squares

Add the transitions to the slide data block in two more columns to the right of the time values – and extend the block definition to include them.

Making a slideshow

Graph Names	Seconds	Trans.	Speed	
BUDGET92	15	4	2	{Fast wipe from left}
DEPTA	10	11	8	{Middling iris close}
DEPTB	10	13	16	{Slow scroll up}
DEBTS	2			{No more graphs}

Explore them and see what you think. A variety of transition styles will certainly help to enliven a presentation, though the flashier ones – stripes, spiral and dissolves – can be over-used. The object of the transitions is to alert people to a new screen. They should not themselves become the focus of attention.

Sound effects
On a PC!? Well, in theory, but unless your PC has an added sound board, they are not worth the effort. The effects are produced from special files, supplied with Quattro Pro. My version came with three: DRUMS.SND, THANKS.SND and FANFARE.SND. Check that you have files with a .SND extension in your Quattro directory, and make a note of their names. To add them to the presentation, type the sound filename in full, in a fifth column of the slide data block. It is played when the graph is first displayed.

Graph Names	Seconds	Trans.	Speed	Sound
BUDGET92	15	4	2	FANFARE.SND
DEPTA	10	11	8	
DEPTB	10	13	16	THANKS.SND
DEBTS	2			DRUMS.SND

Button-controlled presentations
The Annotator lets you define any text element as a *graph button* and link this to another graph or a macro. When the annotated graph is viewed, the button can be 'pressed' by clicking on it, or by pressing its initial letter. (The background can also be defined as a 'button' to link in an error-trapping graph, in case the user misses the target with the mouse.) The system will then display

the linked graph, or run the macro. A graph may have any number of buttons, any number of graphs may be cross-linked via buttons, and the macros may be used to run slideshows. It means that you can build as complex a presentation as you like, with multiple branches and sequences. These could be used for teaching, for exhibitions, for the selective presentation of material during meetings and in other interactive situations.

Defining graph buttons

This is a bit fiddly – more so than should have been the case – since you cannot define a new text element as a button without selecting it first.

1 Sort out your basic graphs first! They must exist before you can create links to them. Make the first graph current.

2 Take the graph off to the Annotator.

3 Select the Text tool, set its properties and write the label.

4 Go into **Pick** mode and select the new text element. Press [F3] or click on the Property area and select **Graph Button**.

5 Give the name of the graph to be called up by the button. If you want more buttons on the graph, return to step 3.

6 Quit the Annotator and save the graph with **Graph I Name Create**. View and check that it looks right and works.

7 If buttons are to be put on other graphs, select the graph with **Graph I Name Display**, then return to step 2.

PART ELEVEN

Customising the system

■SECTION 49
Keystroke shortcuts

In their relentless quest to make life ever easier for the user, the Quattro programmers came up with 'shortcuts' – [Ctrl] key combinations that instantly call up commands from the depths of the menu system. These cut down the number of keystrokes or mouse movements, reducing, for example, the four needed for **Style | Numeric Format** to a single [Ctrl]-[F]. Fewer keystrokes does mean fewer opportunities for mis-keying, though equally a wrongly selected shortcut gets you much deeper into the wrong menus and will take more [Escape]s to cancel. In practice, shortcuts work well if they are regularly used, but it is otherwise safer and as quick to work from the menus.

The pre-assigned shortcuts

Sixteen shortcuts are pre-assigned by the system, and cover those commands that most people will use most often. For the most part they use the initial of the last name in the command, which tends to be the one that best describes the operation. [Ctrl]-[S], for instance, calls up **File | Save** – the **S**ave operation.

One of the set is unusual in that it does not replace a command key sequence. [Ctrl]-[D] is what must be pressed before entering a data value into the sheet. It is also unusual in that it cannot be changed. All the other shortcuts can be re-assigned to different command sequences, if you choose.

[Ctrl]-[A]	Style	Alignment
[Ctrl]-[C]	Edit	Copy
[Ctrl]-[D]	Date prefix – invariable
[Ctrl]-[E]	Edit	Erase block
[Ctrl]-[F]	Style	Numeric Format
[Ctrl]-[G]	Graph	Fast Graph
[Ctrl]-[I]	Edit	Insert
[Ctrl]-[M]	Edit	Move
[Ctrl]-[N]	Edit	Search & Replace	Next

■ SECTION 49
Keystroke shortcuts

[Ctrl]-[P]	Edit I Search & Replace I Previous
[Ctrl]-[R]	Window I Move/Size
[Ctrl]-[S]	File I Save
[Ctrl]-[T]	Window I Tile
[Ctrl]-[W]	Style I Column Width
[Ctrl]-[X]	File I eXit
[Ctrl]-[F10]	Database I Paradox Access I Go

Creating shortcuts

Setting up your own shortcuts is not difficult, and there are ten letter keys still free. Take note of those operations that you use frequently and that are not covered by the default set, then create the shortcuts like this:

1 Work through the menu system to the point where the target command name is highlighted – but not yet selected.

2 Hold [Ctrl] and press [Return].

3 Hold [Ctrl] and press the key letter for the shortcut.

That's it. The shortcut is automatically stored in the system without further ado. Next time that menu is on screen, you will see that the Ctrl-letter combination has been written beside the command name.

You cannot re-assign an existing shortcut without first cancelling its previous use. To do this, work through the menus as in step 1. above, then press [Ctrl]-[Return], followed by two presses on [Delete].

■ SECTION 49
Keystroke shortcuts

Working regularly with Quattro, I have found it useful to create these shortcuts. Like the pre-assigned set, they mainly use initials. Someday, I may find a use for H, J, Q and Z.

[Ctrl]-[B]	Style ǀ Block Widths ǀ Set Width
[Ctrl]-[K]	Edit ǀ Name ǀ Create
[Ctrl]-[L]	Style ǀ Line Drawing
[Ctrl]-[O]	File ǀ Open
[Ctrl]-[U]	File ǀ Utilities ǀ File Manager
[Ctrl]-[V]	Edit ǀ Values
[Ctrl]-[Y]	Edit ǀ Delete

■ SECTION 50
Setting the options

The Options menu offers almost limitless opportunities for tweak-ing the system. Fortunately, the default tweaking is so good that most of them can be happily ignored. There are, however, a few things that should be done fairly early on, and some others that are worth thinking about later. What follows is a selective skim through the Options menu.

Use **Update** if you have changed any of the optional settings and want to keep them. Fail to update, and the system will revert to the default settings when next you start it up.

Hardware
Printers: unless you have an extremely unusual model, installing a parallel printer should present no problems – just pick the Type and Model from the huge range available. With a serial printer, check the communications settings – Baud Rate, Parity, etc. – in the printer manual, and reset them if necessary.

Colors
Quattro gives you control over every single use of colour throughout the system. Changes are put into effect immediately so that – on the main screen at least – you can tell if they work. Some combinations definitely don't work, but if you want to revert to the originals you have only to choose...

Palettes: these store the default colour schemes. There are four possibilities: Colour, Monochrome, Black & White and Grey Scales.

International
These options control those modes of display that vary from country to country. Set your **Currency** symbol, **Punctuation** for numbers, and **Date** and **Time** displays.

■SECTION 50
Setting the options

Startup

This is a bit of a mixed bag and not particularly well named. Yes, these options are operational from start-up time – but then, so are all the rest. However, this set does contain some crucial options.

Directory. Where are your worksheet files stored? If you just stuff them into the Quattro directory, it will become increasingly difficult to find any given file as their numbers mount. Far better to create separate directories for each aspect of your work, then use this option to set as a default that directory which you use most often.

The **Beep** can be turned off, thank heavens. The error messages make it quite clear enough when things have gone wrong, without this irritating intrusion.

The **File Extension** that you set here will be added to the name as you save a sheet. It is normally .WQ1, but there are other possibilities. Set it to .WK1 or .WKS if the sheets are to be passed across to a Lotus 1-2-3 or Symphony user. (Quattro will happily load .WK? files.)

If you set the extension to .WQ!, then the sheet will be saved in the compressed **SQZ!** format. This reduces demands on disks, but has some drawbacks (see below).

The **Menu Tree** option is only really there for hardened 1-2-3 users, or those recently transferred from the early Quattro system. The normal Quattro menu tree is far superior to either alternative. And note that if you do go for the **123** option, there is no way back from its menus!

Other

Another mixed bag! Three of these may be of interest.

Undo should be Enabled, but by default is not. Mistakes happen all too often, and this will let you reverse the effect of an action. There is a small loss of speed if Undo is enabled, but the benefits must outweigh this for most users.

Expanded Memory has slower access time than main memory, but its use does permit more and larger spreadsheets to be run. Quattro normally works on a compromise, storing spreadsheet data in expanded memory and the format data in conventional memory. With massive sheets, opt for both forms of data to be held in expanded memory. For faster operations, opt for either the Format data alone, or None to be held in expanded memory.

Clock watchers may like to have the time displayed at the bottom of the screen. Others may find it distracting.

SQZ! options

These are set on the **File I Utilities SQZ!** menu.

Remove Blanks also removes the formats from the blank cells, which can be a nuisance if more data is to be added later.

Storage of Values can be Exact – to 15 digits; Approximate – to 7 digits; or Removed. In the latter case, the only values that are removed are those generated by formulae. They are then recalculated when the sheet is loaded – causing a delay on startup.

There are two **Versions** of SQZ!. **SQZ! Plus** gives more efficient compression, but the plain version is compatible with the Lotus compression utilities.

Index

Index

Index

Index

Y

Y-Axis, in graphs, 108

Commands

\Data I Query, 219
\Data I Query Extract, 225
\Data I Query Locate, 220
\Data I Sort, 227
\Edit I Copy, 44
\Edit I Delete, 58
\Edit I Erase, 32
\Edit I Fill, 119
\Edit I Insert, 57
\Edit I Move, 60
\Edit I Name Create, 63
\Edit I Name options, 65
\Edit I Values, 47
\File I Close, 56, 177
\File I Close All, 177
\File I Directory, 55
\File I Erase, 38
\File I Exit, 56
\File I New, 56, 177
\File I Open, 55, 176
\File I Retrieve, 54
\File I Save, 52
\File I Save All, 177
\File I Save As, 54
\File I Workspace Restore, 177
\File I Workspace Save, 177
\Graph menu, 90
\Graph I Fast Graph, 90
\Graph I Name Slide, 241
\Options menu, 249
\Options I Recalculate Iterations, 168
\Print menu, 81
\Print I Graph Print, 111

\Style menu, 68
\Tools I Combine, 232
\Tools I Extract, 189
\Tools I Solve For, 170
\Tools I Update Links, 175
\Tools I What If, 162
\Windows I Map View, 182
\Windows I Move/Size, 180
\Windows I Stack, 179
\Windows I Tile, 178
\Windows I Zoom, 179

Functions

@AVG, 154
@HLOOKUP, 128
@IF, 124
@INDEX, 130
@IPAYMT, 143
@IRATE, 142
@MIN, 163
@NOW, 76
@NPER, 142
@PAYMT, 141
@PPAYMT, 143
@PVAL, 142
@SUM, 27
@TODAY, 75
@VLOOKUP, 128

Macro Commands

{?}, 208
{BRANCH ...}, 210
{GETLABEL ...}, 208
{GETNUMBER ...}, 208
{GRAPHCHAR ...}, 209
{IF ...}, 210
{MENUBRANCH ...}, 210
{MESSAGE ...}, 209